I will always remember the moment I learned that Geordie Stewart had successfully reached the summit of Everest. It was an extraordinary achievement from an exceptional young man, and St Andrews rejoiced in his success.

In Search of Sisu is a blisteringly honest account of what it took to make it to the top. Inspiring and surprising by turn, each page bears testimony to Geordie's courage, determination and resilience.

— PROFESSOR LOUISE RICHARDSON, VICE-CHANCELLOR OF THE UNIVERSITY OF OXFORD

ANDREW,
WHAT A GREAT FEW YEARS WE'VE
HAD! I LOOK FORWARD TO MORE
SHARED ADVENTURES IN THE
FUTURE. Geordie

IN SEARCH OF SISU

A PATH TO CONTENTMENT VIA THE HIGHEST POINT ON EVERY CONTINENT

GEORDIE STEWART

Sisu is a concept that lies at the core of Finnish culture and national identity. It has a unique meaning, roughly translated into English as grit, inner courage and determination in the face of adversity.

To my family, for always believing and never doubting.

To Dorje, Heidi and Jonny for teaching me the values of peace, kindness and love.

FOREWORD

I first met a young Geordie Stewart in Kathmandu airport. Like so many groups, we were busying ourselves with the various logistics and the somewhat awkward niceties of small talk to complete strangers. I use the word awkward as the type of characters often attracted to adventure holidays, and particularly to the extreme, are seldom considered normal. They are often restless souls, searching for something, with an inner drive on a quest for purpose. They can sit in a busy room and feel lonely. They judge themselves on their own scale and chase a sense of achievement and feeling of self-worth that is otherwise missing. Psychologists have long studied these types, linking foundations to childhood. We used to call them eccentrics or characters and for those who found a medium to successfully channel such drive, be it in sport, feats of adventure, business achievements or acts of bravery, we would laud them as heroes. Others may know them as misfits, self-focused or distracted.

To those who seek adventure, particularly in high mountains, the question often asked is: 'Why?' For many, George

Mallory symbolised the British colonial spirit of gentlemanly adventure, being notoriously eccentric and famously climbing in a tweed jacket, Jermyn Street shirt and hobnail boots. His story of adventure is the last of the great age and is both romantic and one of the great unsolved mysteries. His answer was 'Because it's there!' ... and for me, alongside the likes of Shackleton, Brummie Stokes, Paddy Maine and Captain Oates, he was a hero. When I met Geordie, he was well-spoken with plans for Sandhurst, the Cavalry and dreams of adventure. As we were also hoping to summit Everest on the less popular north side, following the 1920s British expedition route, I couldn't help being reminded of Mallory.

Bedtime stories of valour and gallantry are what we all revel in, yet stories are crafted and sometimes embellished. The reality of life and especially climbing mountains is perfunctory and far less glamorous; so the strength of someone's 'why' becomes important, especially when the going gets tough. It can be unique and is, of course, hugely personal. Many of those who venture to the mountains don't have a reason before they leave but hope to find one once they are there.

This book is therefore not about climbing but about growing up. A very personal, courageous and reflective journey of someone's transition from boy into man and about finding themselves. In doing so it also illustrates that by finding purpose, people can achieve their dreams. As Walter Bonatti once wrote: *'Mountains are the means, the man is the end. The goal is not to reach the tops of mountains, but to improve the man.'*

Josh Lewsey MBE

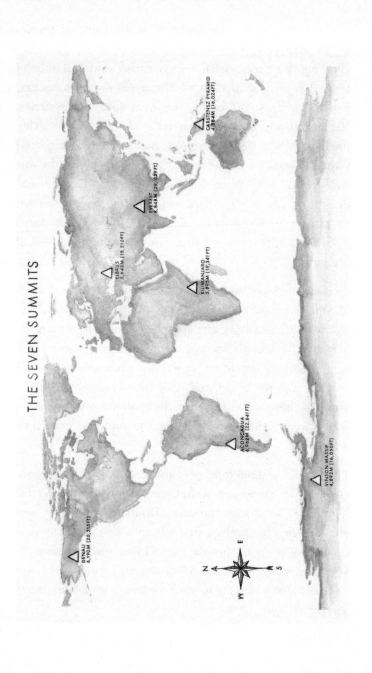

THE SEVEN SUMMITS

DENALI
6,190M (20,310FT)

ELBRUS
5,642M (18,510FT)

EVEREST 8,848M (29,029FT)

KILIMANJARO
5,895M (19,341FT)

CARSTENSZ PYRAMID
4,884M (16,024FT)

ACONCAGUA
6,962M (22,841FT)

VINSON MASSIF
4,892M (16,050FT)

N
W   E
S

PROLOGUE

MY HEART WAS POUNDING DUE TO FEAR AND PHYSICAL exertion. My lungs cried out, thirsty for any oxygen they could find. I removed my mask to see if it was restricting the flow of air, pleading for something to give, but nothing came back and I replaced the mask to calm myself as much as possible.

Don't look down, don't look down, I kept telling myself, then chose to ignore my own advice. Attached to one of the ropes I was about to clip onto was the dead body of a climber. Lying at the bottom of the Second Step, at a height of 8,610m, he wore the same boots as me and a similar down suit. I had been warned of this but the situation was too much.

I was scared for my life.

It was the first body I had ever seen. My legs wobbled and shook uncontrollably as my mind raced. I kept saying *I don't want to die. I don't want to be in that position.* I was isolated and exposed.

I tried to adjust my focus upwards. I stepped away from the ledge and towards the ladder. I was given a moment to reflect on my options as two climbers descended, then I clipped in and made the choice to keep going. One rung at a time before I hauled my way to the top of this imposing obstacle.

To my surprise, I then encountered another stricken teammate with two empty oxygen bottles alongside him. With a fresh supply from another climber, he managed to descend and on I continued in a fatigued daze. Our team leader passed me about 10 minutes later. I was worried he would assess my state and tell me to stop. Instead, he reminded me of our turnaround time and let me proceed upwards.

I was scared, alone, and without a radio. *What was I doing?*

Only 150m to go now. I could see the Third Step; I could see the summit slopes. I was higher than any other mountain in the world.

The end was in sight and so onwards I laboured. At this altitude, my mind was slowing down. I was in a hazy world of self-doubt and summit focus. All I could motivate myself to do was put one foot in front of the other. My body was screaming at me to yield, to give in to the pain and exhaustion; to give up. I could not shake the thought of just calling it quits and heading back down to safety but something deep within was compelling me to move. I needed to find *sisu*. I needed that inner courage and determination. I needed that extra level of psychological strength to not stop.

All the drama was behind me now. I had climbed through the dark without ropes or a head torch. I had seen a Sherpa accepting his own death and witnessed a teammate suffering from frozen eyeballs. I had seen a human speaking to his rucksack as if to another person and another stranded in the 'Death Zone' having run out of oxygen.

It was now just a personal war waging between my ears about how much I wanted to make the top. I knew what I had sacrificed to get here and this was my one chance. It was now or never.

I encountered a Sherpa who told me the summit was four hours away. It was 9 a.m. and our turnaround time was in two hours. I knew the risks that lay ahead as a solo and relatively inexperienced climber without support or radio communications. I knew that my energy reserves were depleting by the minute.

Equally, I had obsessed about reaching the summit of Everest for years and this was my only chance. Only 150m more and I would realise my dream of standing on top of the world. It was decision time.

1

Daydreaming

Those who dream by night in the dusty recesses of their minds wake in the day to find that it was vanity: but the dreamers of the day are dangerous men, for they may act their dreams with open eyes, to make it possible.

T.E. Lawrence

Exploring in nature is something I have always loved. That liberating spirit of adventure and thirst to see the world has been with me since I was a child. Not exploring in the sense of discovering new lands but rather experiencing the beauty of our natural surroundings. The simple joy of watching the dew rise on winter mornings or sitting on a hillside and seeing the setting sun descend over the mountaintops.

Throughout my childhood, I ventured around the Scottish Highlands with my dad and his passion for the outdoors has trickled into my psyche. We ascended hills of varying sizes, in varying conditions that stretched, even at an early age, my concept of achieving something that initially seemed out of my grasp. I summited Ben Nevis before my teenage years and remember stubbornly refusing to admit my levels of exhaustion. Knowing this, Dad would diplomatically request a rest every so often, recognising my pre-pubescent machismo.

I slightly lost that simple satisfying joy of adventure when I was a teenager. The distractions of growing up, of social recognition and sporting achievement took precedent. Despite being reasonable at school, I did not stand out. I had early promise in sports and athletics, particularly running, but had somewhat plateaued.

Before settling into university life, I planned a year out but was strangely uninspired. Despite having an open-ended opportunity to discover the world, I felt more comfortable with the idea of adhering to the successful formula of those before me. Following the crowd seemed to be a rewarding path and the quest for purpose, to 'find yourself', in the company of other teenagers was apparently a necessary step prior to university. I planned to work for six months in odd jobs and save enough money to fly to Canada, be a ski instructor, and then go to Central America to travel. It was meant to help you become more mature and independent. It should have ticked all the boxes – combining travel, personal growth, and a blank canvas to plot a route. Something within my spirit, however, remained unfulfilled by the plan I had lined up.

When I was aged 10, Bear Grylls gave a talk at my school about his successful Everest attempt. I had not followed his ventures since, but that initial lecture using a temperamental overheard projector had stuck in my head and I am convinced my subconscious kept the memory for a reason. Dad gave me Bear's book, *Facing Up,* when I was 17 and something about it struck a chord. His humility, vulnerability and willingness to persevere were traits I admired. His focus to keep a goal in mind and, despite setbacks, finally stand on top of the world, aged 23, was unique.

Like many aspirational teenagers, I drew parallels between his life and mine. However, more than most, I saw something that drew me. I did not merely gloss over the words before moving onto the next thing. The words on the page represented something more than just someone else's achievement: the book symbolised something for me to set my mind on. Reading that book opened my eyes. An alternative path emerged providing a genuine challenge, plus the promise of fulfilment and uniqueness that was lacking from the well-trodden path.

I was meant to be revising for my final exams at the time, but an Everest-shaped seed had been sown, and I delved straight into the internet to research everything I could. Within a matter of days, I had amassed reams of articles and facts about *Sagarmatha*, as it is known in Nepal, or *Chomolungma*, as it is known in Tibet, 'Goddess Mother of the World'. I knew the climbing statistics, weather windows, summit success rates and the stories of the early pioneers. I compulsively watched every Everest documentary and video clip that I could find online. I watched Bear Grylls' *Born Survivor* show on Discovery Channel to further my understanding of survival. I purchased iconic Everest texts, from

Jon Krakauer's *Into Thin Air,* written about the 1996 disaster, to Edmund Hillary's *High Adventure* about the first successful ascent of the mountain in 1953. I had become a hugely passionate, secretive, and, crucially, inexperienced mountaineer.

Andrew Carnegie said, 'If you want to be happy, set a goal that commands your thoughts, liberates your energy and inspires your hopes.' While researching Everest, and the associated difficulties involved, I happened across the 'Seven Summits' – a challenge that involves climbing the highest mountain on every continent across the globe. Again, my interest was piqued. Travelling to every continent, for seven different climbs culminating in summiting Mount Everest? I was sold. I researched further about the times of year to climb, the expected costs, who to climb with and what kit was required. An ambitious new adventure was unfurling before me. I saw potential and felt focus the like of which I had not previously encountered. That month would change the course of my life.

After finishing school, I seriously discussed this absurd idea with Dad for the first time. His response was supportive. 'It's certainly ambitious,' he said 'There's a lot of luck and pitfalls that potentially await but, knowing you Geord, I support you fully and have faith you will achieve it.' I waited a bit longer before letting Mum and my sisters into this little world of mine. After hearing my plan, despite the anxious and curious first line of enquiry, they realised it was clear in my mind and placed themselves fully behind me. The project at this point became a team effort, something it would remain for years to come.

I had already made notes for each of the seven expeditions including dates, costs and technical requirements. I immediately sent this document to my family for their own awareness and to try and dispel their fears. It came like a whirlwind and perhaps they thought this was just another phase that would pass. I knew it represented more than that. My desire to climb the Seven Summits was an ambition based on the natural allure of mountains and an inner voice telling me that Everest represented the ultimate goal I sought. On a deeper level, climbing the Seven Summits was probably also my way of aiming to achieve something of significance, and discovering a sense of self away from the parameters of the norm.

I made a rough calculation that to achieve my pre-university aims, I would need about £10,000. I needed to pay for kit, a basic mountaineering course, an expedition to South America and then, finally, an expedition to Russia. Nobody was willing or able to fund this for me so I made the decision to forego a social life and dedicate my time to raising money. For six months over the summer I worked Monday to Friday on minimum wage, putting up marquees and racking up pretty significant hours. At weekends, I worked for catering companies at parties and weddings. Through living at home with minimal expenses, and sacrificing the social life most of my mates were enjoying, I managed to save enough money to begin this journey.

On a friend's recommendation, I visited a climbing shop in Hampshire run by a guy called Steve. His enthusiasm and willingness to assist was beyond what I could have imagined. He helped not because he saw a potential customer (although this is what he got), but rather because he saw an ambitious and naïve boy, about to embark on a tumultuous journey. The knowledge I gained was invaluable, and I made the two-hour round trip countless times before I departed. Visiting Steve's little shop became part of my pre- and post-expedition ritual for the next four years.

I learned voraciously by expanding my mountaineering bookshelf and devouring all the information I could find online. My theoretical knowledge was becoming dispropor-tionately strong compared to my still non-existent practical understanding of high altitude. I could explain the distressing and unrelenting symptoms of altitude sickness. I could explain the impatience of being stuck in a storm at high camp, unable to move up or down. And yet, up till now I had experienced nothing of the sort.

As the autumn and winter months rolled in, the demand for marquees waned so I took on a handful of jobs that enabled me to prolong my insular working routine and continue to save money. I was gardening, interior decorating and working in a bathroom accessories warehouse packing and sealing boxes of soap holders and sink plungers. I experi-enced the financial motivation of working for commission for the first time at a call centre answering debt-manage-ment queries in response to a government message. By December, I had squirrelled away enough money to proceed with the first part of my ambition. This was part one of a fairly cavalier plan – deciding I wanted to climb the highest mountain on every continent and then working out how to do it.

2

ACONCAGUA

6,962m / 22,841ft

Climbing a mountain represents a chance to briefly free oneself of the small concerns of our common lives, to strip off nonessentials, to come down to the core of life itself.

Mateo Cabello

I lied on my application form to attempt Aconcagua. As the highest mountain outside the Himalayas, some previous high altitude experience is a prerequisite. It is often seen as a logical next step after Kilimanjaro, but at just under 7,000m it is a challenge not to be underestimated. I had learned to climb properly in Scotland a matter of weeks before, but claimed I had done 4,000m ascents in the Alps. For an 18-year-old with little experience, but high ambitions, it was a bold strategy.

Learning to climb in Scotland on a two-week winter mountaineering course had been eye-opening. My guide, Zac, was
informative and understanding. He knew I had Aconcagua
booked. He had seen ambitious youngsters with fleeting
dreams come and go through the Scottish hills. I was fit and
determined, but when it came to awareness and pragmatism
on the mountains, I was woefully short on expertise.

Prior to Aconcagua, I had never been on a proper expedition so I went into it both excited and wary. I recall getting to
Heathrow and feeling like a fraud as I met the rest of the
team. They were older, more experienced, and had mountaineering yarns to spin. I bid farewell to Mum and was now
fending for myself properly for the first time. It was a
welcoming and like-minded group of strangers, but it was a
big step into the unknown for me, and a steep learning
curve was about to begin.

After the tedium of sorting visas, establishing logistics and
deciphering the Argentinian transport network, we finally
started to move. The trek into the mountain was a joy as
our team of 12 meandered our way through the valley floor.
This was it: I was now underway in my Seven Summits
attempt. Everything was new to me, from staying in huts
overnight, trying to embrace the local culture and
language, to making small talk about climbing without
displaying my ignorance. As we slowly gained altitude I
had Steve's voice in the back of my head saying, 'Take it
slow and drink plenty of water. Never be at the front of the
group, but equally, don't be the one slowing everyone
down. Never be the last one to get ready and keep others

waiting. There are no prizes for winning this particular race.'

The early stages of expeditions are filled with little mind games. We were not competing against each other per se, but nobody wanted to be seen as the weak link. People are almost putting a marker down in the sand about their capability and speed before moving with the rest of the group. I had to actively resist the urge to be near the front – the clichéd teenager bolting off implied naivety, something I was desperate to hide. After four sunshine-filled days, we reached Base Camp at around 4,500m. I attempted to brush off my headache to our guide, Adam, but he could probably see straight through me. Overall, my health was reasonable and, given the fib on my initial form, I was unable to share this altitude personal best.

Alpenglow permitted only the summit of Aconcagua an essence of light and, 2,500m above me, I was curious as to what it would be like. I was excited to stretch my limits and prove people wrong. I enjoyed the fact that I was out here on my own little project. I was relieved that I felt a sense of purpose and focus while on the mountain. At the time, I was not overly bothered by the route or the views we might encounter. I just looked up at the top and wanted to be there. Aged 18, all I wanted was to reach the highest point in South America.

Here began the process of acclimatisation, of climbing high and sleeping low. This would enable our bodies to produce the requisite red blood cells to cope with the change of oxygen levels in the atmosphere. The human body is not designed for high altitude; we have to give it time to adapt. The process was simple. We trekked up to Camp 1, cached some kit and food for higher up the mountain, and moved back down to Base Camp again, to rest and recover.

We moved as a team but, even with my limited experience, I felt the compulsion to move at my own speed. Some people found added motivation from others behind, or in front, but I felt restricted by it. That's not to say I would go quicker or slower but at least I could determine the rhythm that suited my body best. For the first time I saw how, by removing my mind from the immediate situation and the discomfort I was in, I was able to make genuine progress with far less energy expended while allowing my thoughts to roam free.

I was constantly learning, and absorbing as much knowledge as these wiser climbers alongside me could give. I remember Adam saying, 'Prepare for the worst and hope for the best.' It is a simple mantra, and one I have certainly fallen foul of since, but the principle involves as much mental preparation as physical. That's why training needs to be hard. If you train with mud, sweat and tears then that's what your body and mind know they can cope with.

———

Climbing requires you to look out for the safety and well-being of teammates, in the knowledge that they will do the same for you. The selfish man on a climbing team is quickly brought back down to earth. Putting up a tent, boiling water, moving shared kit and equipment are all done more efficiently when done as a group. The best teammates and climbers do the right thing, as opposed to the easy thing, because it benefits everyone.

Beyond the knowledge I was gaining about climbing at high

altitude, I was also learning a huge amount about successful team cohesion on an expedition. I fell afoul of this on a couple of occasions. I needed to learn the value of silence and letting the small things pass – everyone has their isms in life. I was young and still quite prickly in character. I needed to learn to balance my emotions when in an intense environment. I learned that sometimes the best path was the one of least resistance and that I needed to be able to let things slide if I wanted to remain a valued and trusted member of the team.

Halfway through the expedition, we made the decision to traverse the mountain as a team. This meant moving all our kit and equipment up one side of the mountain, and back down the other, as opposed to retracing our steps. There were obvious problems to this, namely a fiendishly arduous move with kit piled up high and excess equipment hanging off the sides of our rucksacks. It wasn't a pretty sight but it did the trick and we all managed to make it to High Camp.

I felt stronger as the trip went on. That heavy day in particular, I switched something in my head that accepted this was *the* day to perform and to prove to my teammates, and myself, that I was ready. While others were battling against the debilitating effects of high altitude, I felt content with my levels of hydration and nourishment.

Calories are burnt at a disproportionate rate at altitude compared with at sea level. The body is attempting to produce more red blood cells, and the heart rate is constantly higher than at sea level, to cope with the thinning air, which raises the body's basal metabolic rate. Added to this, the calories expended through the sheer amount of time spent exercising is far greater than one normally trains for. Despite this, while others sought maximum calories per gram, I looked at the ingredients of foods and set aside the items with high fat and calorific content. I would consume what I deemed *enough* to proceed, but never more than was necessary. I actually enjoyed the fact that I would be losing quite so much weight in such a short space of time. I knew that what I was doing was undermining my overall performance, and chances of summiting, but my prudence was in a losing battle against my fractured mind.

Come summit day, there were more lessons to learn. Setting off and moving in the dark with a head torch was new to me. I was fearful of the cold and decided to double up on gloves and socks for the opening stint. Several hours in, my fingers and toes had become increasingly sore. In an odd way, despite the discomfort, this was reassuring as I was told you should only really begin to panic when you can't feel any pain. When the team stopped for a quick break at sunrise, our barmy but wonderful Argentinian guide, Caesar, took action. He was spinning my arms around, slapping my fingers and toes and then, to my surprise, made me remove a pair of gloves and socks. I have since learned it is important to have a pocket of air between the end of your toes and boots. This gradually warms up, or at least doesn't get as cold as a snug fit, thus minimising the risk of frostbite.

Relieved and re-energised, we progressed upwards at a reasonable pace in fairly benign conditions. We had a strong team but two guys did not start the day as they'd had to descend from High Camp with bad altitude sickness. It was a tough, but correct, decision by Adam. He showed the moral courage to stand by his conviction in what was right for the overall success of the team. By the time we reached our final checkpoint, we knew that we just had to meander our way around a scree slope and then traverse along the summit ridge. I was bloody excited. I felt, with almost total certainty, that we would make the top. When I could see the final ledge to the summit plateau, I waited before giving Caesar a hug and joining the rest of the team. I knew Caesar was proud of me. I was his youngest ever client in over twenty expeditions. I think he saw my vulnerability, and desire to reach the summit, as a project that he had become emotionally invested in.

Regardless of its height, the summit of a mountain is special. The amount of time struggling to get there is illogical given the moments spent on the top. It is a perplexing paradox, but the emotive power of those moments justifies the pain of getting there.

We were standing not only at the highest point in South America, but also the highest point outside of the Himalayas. The summit gave us the opportunity to savour a glorious view as Argentina and Chile sprawled beneath us. I was totally overwhelmed and didn't really know what to do. Being there was the greatest thing I had achieved in my life so far. I took a brief, and irritatingly amateur, video showing my youth, overwhelming joy and emotion.

I did not really feel any yearning to celebrate wildly. I felt more of a sense of deep pride and satisfaction. I had a little cry upon reflecting how the past year had led to this moment. It's easy to narrow expeditions to the few weeks spent on the mountain itself. For me, at that point, it was the psychological and emotional haze I was trying to overcome in the rest of my life that had transfused itself to the top of this mountain. I took some memorable pictures with my team and felt – as I still feel – genuine pride in having achieved that summit with them. It was a special moment.

I probably misjudged my levels of genuine exhaustion, so focused had I been on the importance of getting to the top. Consequently, I experienced a significant drop in my energy levels on the descent. It was the first time *sisu* was taking centre stage. *Sisu* required me to dig quite deep to motivate myself to keep going. I knew I would get down to High Camp in the end. I had no genuine fear for my own safety, and had made reasonable time, but it was the first time I had really tested my limits. I required *sisu* to really push me beyond the boundaries of my perceived mental and physical capacity.

Sisu isn't necessarily about your physical strength but rather what's going on between your ears. It is fighting the inner voice pleading with you to give up, to sit down and take a break. It is that part of your conscience that is demanding, against every other instinct in your body, you make damned sure to keep putting one foot in front of the other.

I successfully made it to High Camp in the afternoon and slumped down next to my tent. I looked back up at the mountain with joyous satisfaction and relief. I was safe. I had done it.

That evening I made another bad decision by drinking cele-bratory whisky from a hip flask that Dad gave me for the event of a successful attempt. Given my serious dehydration, heavy exhaustion and a headache, the effects were acutely noticeable. It was as though a hangover hit me before any of the gratifying effects of alcohol had chance to make an impact. Needless to say, this was not to be repeated. The following day, a weary and unglamorous descent to Base Camp ensued. A tedious scree slope descent was gratefully concluded with a ceremonial discarding of all waste, human and packaged, which we had carried for the previous few weeks on the outside of our rucksacks, into a centralised bin.

After a night of sipping Dioralyte to counter my headache, we were on our way trekking home from the mountain. Eight out of 10 members of the group had made the summit. The expedition was definitely a success overall, and testament to our strength as a team. On mountaineering expeditions, there is often only a brief opportunity to grasp success due to weather windows and logistics. The key appeared to be in maximising one's health, and thus the chance of success, when it mattered most.

Returning to civilisation after the expedition was a joy as spirits were high, the weight of expectation and pressures had been released and a mood of genuine relaxation emerged. We took pride – though not unmixed with embarrassment – in the fact that the hotel porters sprayed air freshener in the lobby after our departure. We could now socialise in Mendoza with plentiful supplies of Malbec wine, and gaze admiringly at its beautiful and unattainable residents. These final moments are, in their own way, memories as treasured as those on the mountainside.

My immediate celebrations, though, took a turn for the

worse. On my way back to the hotel after dinner, I was happily minding my own business when a brick was smashed in my face and the pockets ripped off my shorts as I ran away from three locals in hot pursuit. Thankfully the months of training and the benefits of high altitude assisted my escape. I was eventually halted by a group of teenagers who took compassion on me.

The picture I took shows tearful eyes and crimson blood streaming down my face. Before long, I was in hospital receiving 12 stitches to my battered nose and mouth. Adam had been called, and was a calming, parent-like presence before I was interviewed by the police. My first exposure to the media took place as local papers and radio were ravenous for a story about a young British climber attacked in the city centre. The suitably shocking photo accompanying the story added to the drama and gave me a brilliant newspaper cutting to keep.

My poor mum's emotions were torn as we spoke on the phone for the first time: delighted to hear of my successful attempt, horrified at what had happened afterwards. Instead of gorging on Argentinian rump steak, I was reduced to drinking soup through a straw and unable to speak properly as a result of the swelling and stitches.

One of the beauties of these expeditions is the degree of simplicity and escapism one achieves. It is something I have learned to appreciate more as my experience has increased, and the stress of jobs and relationships has mounted: that desire for freedom, to transcend the reality of day-to-day life. On expeditions, you are reduced to living out of a rucksack and sleeping in a tent for weeks and months on end. You're cluttered and uncomfortable a lot of the time, while your personal space is woefully imposed upon. Yet you can be totally at ease with the environment and at peace within it.

Aconcagua taught me the wonders of sitting outside my tent in a down jacket and watching the sunset in silence. It taught me the value of discretion, and of letting other people's idiosyncrasies slide, as they no doubt reciprocated the sentiments. Crucially, it taught me about humility and teamwork. It provided an informative insight into the value of cohesion with others. Aged 18, with minimal experience, I went into the trip proud yet vulnerable, ignorant yet arrogant; through experience, I had matured and further fuelled my passion for this challenge.

3

KILIMANJARO

5,895m / 19,341ft

Have the courage to follow your heart and intuition. They somehow already know what you truly want to become.

Steve Jobs

Within a week of returning from Argentina, I was back at work and saving money. I paid the deposit to climb the highest mountain in Europe, Elbrus, in August, and had several months to secure the rest. The wandering soul in me had another plan, one I had concocted with a friend many months before. In March, I flew to Bangkok for several months travelling abroad, to tick the gap-year box, before returning for Elbrus.

The hedonistic yearnings of teenagers exploring the world,

and embracing their new-found freedom, in Thailand was a world away from the life I had been living. I had such a clear goal and focus on what I wanted to achieve, and had been sufficiently disciplined to make it materialise.

It was impossible explaining to people my insular experiences over the past year. My struggles in raising the money, my experiences with *sisu* on the expedition, the personal battle I was having in my mind. I was with an old friend but something wasn't right. I was plagued by the financial guilt of my decision. I knew every Thai baht I spent was money I could not spend on a new down jacket, a visa to climb Elbrus in Russia, or a spare ice axe. I ate almost solely pad thai, one of the cheapest meals on offer, once or twice a day. This was an obsession based as much on the guilt of spending money as it was in regards to my issues with food. I found myself in a group of carefree guys enjoying life, but I felt isolated as I fought these inner pressures. It was self-imposed pressure, of course. Nobody told me to climb or lose weight, but the mounting pressure needed an escape valve.

I managed a feeble 10 days of a 'normal' gap year in Thailand. If my objective was to follow the crowd, I failed dramatically. I was always encouraged to follow my heart, and at that moment, it was blinkered towards the Seven Summits, and instinctively told me to escape as soon as possible. I had time to deliberate on my next decision after a swift flight change, and a 30-hour bus journey, with my old friend Jamie, heading south to Singapore.

Back in the UK in early April, I looked at my bank balance

of £1,000 and had a tinge of regret. Thailand had not cost me that much, but enough to question the decision. If nothing else, it was a life experience and allowed me to re-evaluate my priorities. As Steve Jobs said, 'The things you regret most in life are the things you didn't do.' A thousand pounds could be stretched a long way and I had a browse to see what I could usefully do before Elbrus. Denali in North America was out of my price range and beyond my experience bracket. Everest in Asia, Vinson in Antarctica and Carstensz Pyramid in Australasia/Oceania had similar issues, which left me with one option: Kilimanjaro.

Kilimanjaro is the highest mountain in Africa, standing at 5,895m or 19,341ft. I knew a number of people who had climbed it, and the majority had had reasonable success. Equally, I heard a number of alarming tales of friends who could not remember making the summit as a result of altitude sickness, or who were throwing up near the top. They had been persuaded to plough on at the behest of their guides, who knew the impact of a summit photo when it came to tipping.

My birthday is 5 May, and I decided to book flights with a view to heading out to Tanzania, and welcoming in my 19th birthday on the Roof of Africa. My flights cost £370, leaving me just over £600 to sort accommodation and logistics and then clamber to the top. It was all set to be a fairly impetuous approach, and another set of experiences that would assist in my personal and climbing development.

I had never been to Africa before, so arriving in Nairobi was eye-opening. After a string of intrusive offers at the airport, I eventually found a bus that would take me across the Kenyan border, and on to Arusha, in Tanzania. With people clinging onto the sides, smashed windows, punctures and cramped spaces, the bus journey itself was pretty exciting. I found the cheapest shared room in a backpackers' hostel and from there could prepare for my attempt. Refusing to accept the repeated answer that a solo ascent was not possible, I made my own way to the park entrance. At the gates I was denied access; the rules stipulate the need for a guide with you at all times. Returning to the drawing board, I went to locate a suitable guide to direct me up what was, to my knowledge, a fairly simple route.

Eventually someone recommended a local called Basha, the cousin of the hostel manager. It sounded a bit vague but if it got me to the National Park and a clear shot at Kili, then I was up for it. I explained what was required, and he assured me that he had over 50 successful summits, so I was in safe hands.

Apart from the mountain itself, Tanzania was a wonderful country to visit, awash with optimism and kindness. For a shy and cautious 18-year-old, it was otherworldly but enticing. I did not have the comfort of having a mate alongside me, with whom I could chat about the complexity of the task ahead. But by then I possessed a bit of mountaineering experience, and was confident in my ability to reach the summit, having reached the highest point outside the Himalayas a matter of months before. Without consciously knowing it, I was already underway on the other part of my journey: growing up and understanding who I was.

An advantage of climbing Kilimanjaro is the ease with which one can ascend it due to its limited technical requirements. This allows youngsters, walkers and climbers alike to experience high altitude and enjoy a great sense of achievement. Having wound our way through the forest, we stayed in mountain huts, prepared to head higher, and hopefully catch a glimpse of this famous mountain.

Some mountains in the world are instantly recognisable: the North Face of the Eiger, Mount Fuji, the Matterhorn, Everest, and Kilimanjaro all fit into that category. I had an image in my mind, and I was excited to see the snow-capped summit slopes of this glorious piece of nature. Often the scale and magnitude of a mountain cannot be truly grasped until you are there, struggling on its slopes. Seeing your objective up ahead somehow revitalises one's motivation and you have a brief opportunity to shine under its influence. I have probably shifted my perspective on mountains over the years as I have witnessed their ferocity, yielded to their power and clung on in desperation as they resolutely denied access.

As I progressed upwards, I would daydream and let my imagination roam. Nature has this power of allowing clarity of thought, of stimulating ideas, and providing moments of reflection unavailable in one's living room. The feel of the African heat bearing down, and a gentle breeze whipping up the dust before me, was a comforting sensation, while Kilimanjaro loomed ahead.

Basha reiterated what Kili guides often say, *'pole pole'*, meaning 'slowly slowly', their way of reminding over-excitable, glory-seeking Westerners to relax. To a determined teenager, who naïvely and arrogantly thought, despite the mountain's height, that the challenge would not be of any great significance, the restrained approach was unsettling. I would rush on ahead at my own pace, and allow Basha to saunter behind. My mind never truly detached from my focus on the end goal. I was too set on achieving the summit and don't think I appreciated the rarity and joy of where I was.

After a number of days of gentle trekking, we made our way to High Camp at Kibo Hut. I had been restless earlier that morning, and charged off quicker than necessary. The resulting headache and dehydration from excessive altitude gain in a short time led me to worry that my summit bid could potentially be scuppered. It was a foolish mistake. I tried to remind myself to stay healthy all the way to the final day, that's the one that counts, but ignored my own advice. I hurriedly drank large quantities of water, and thankfully the headache, and my concerns, subsided. We planned for a midnight start, allowing a sunrise summit, before hotfooting it back down the mountain.

At midnight, I turned 19. I reflected it was a peculiar way to spend a birthday but was happy with where I was. I waited for Basha, but had become accustomed to 'Tanzanian Time', so was not really expecting him on the dot. When he did arrive, to my surprise he had forgotten his head torch. Sharing one torch between the two of us, we had no choice but to proceed up the mountain with my torch shining through his legs. Added to this, or as a result, he appeared to be navigating in a somewhat haphazard manner. It's hard to have confidence in a guide who stops, asks for a light, waves it around aimlessly, and then nudges off into the distance. None the wiser, I followed on behind and wondered what might be influencing his route choice. *What would happen if my head torch cut out? And what would have happened if I had also forgotten mine? A pitch black assault? A midday ascent? No ascent perhaps.*

All were interesting thoughts, and convenient ways of distracting my mind. The frustration of following someone who didn't know where they were going was exasperating by now. The constant stops were not helping my body warmth either. The slow pace meant not enough blood was pumping around my body to keep my extremities warm. The body has an impressive way of prioritising one's essential organs – brain, heart, lungs, kidneys and liver – when it is in the extreme cold. The side effect of this means one's fingers and toes are increasingly susceptible to frostbite.

Thankfully, Basha appeared to pick up a scent from some-where, and our progress increased drastically. Raising my heart rate, and renewing my focus, brought some welcome warmth to my digits. Before long, we had reached Gilman's Point at 5,681m, and I knew we were nearing the summit approach. The route to this point had been primarily a steep scree slope, but thankfully the terrain and gradients now became more diverse.

Around six hours after setting off, the beam of my head torch caught a glimpse of the famous sign at the top. Feel-ings of infantile joy and relief swept over my body. It was not the dream-summit view I had envisaged when I set off weeks before, but rather, like on Aconcagua, it induced a deeper sense of satisfaction. I posed for a photo next to the iconic notice, which reads:

CONGRATULATIONS YOU ARE NOW AT UHURU PEAK TANZANIA 5,895m

AFRICA'S HIGHEST POINT WORLD'S LARGEST FREE
STANDING VOLCANO
WELCOME

It was still cold and dark. Basha and I made our way down the mountain and, within half an hour, we were again back at Gilman's Point with the memorable sunrise I hoped for. An orange glow rose above a pillowy blanket of clouds with nothing peeking through. Just the two of us on the Roof of Africa – glorious. Our energy levels then allowed us, after one night at the Horombo Huts (3,705m), to get back to the park entrance, at the Marangu Gate (1,860m), the following morning.

A parallel in the aftermath of my ascents of Aconcagua and Kilimanjaro then emerged. Although climbing the mountain was the main focus, the events following the climb are also seared into my memory. My finances were severely stretched after the park fees, guiding fees, accommodation, food and tips. After returning to Arusha, and trying to withdraw money, my bankcard was declined. I was going to have to get by with the nominal amount of cash left in my wallet. I had a last night at the hostel, and was bought a couple of beers by someone I got chatting to at the bar, something that certainly sent me off into a good night's sleep. All that remained, after buying the bus ticket back to Nairobi, was less than 200 Kenyan shillings, the equivalent of about £1.

I made it to Nairobi and, as the daylight began to fade, I opted against food, and bought as many single cigarettes as possible – a hugely appreciated business concept. I found what appeared to be a quiet part of the city, and wrapped up warm and went to sleep hugging my rucksack, savouring the hunger-negating impact of the nicotine. To my relief, I woke with the sun up and all my kit in place, enquired where the buses departed, and finally made my way to the airport, tired and extremely hungry.

The delivery of free pretzels on the flight allowed me to explain my situation to the air stewardess. She returned with an alarming supply of Gü chocolate brownies and a maternal wink. The floodgates had opened. An eating disorder, combined with a successful summit, and a large calorie deficit, meant that, within a matter of minutes, I had wolfed the lot down; I then felt enormously guilty and extremely ill. Despite my developing levels of self-assurance, this inner battle inside my mind would not subside. I promptly made my way to the toilet, made myself throw up, washed my face, and returned to my seat feeling guilty and saddened at my own failings.

Kilimanjaro was another piece in the puzzle of this complicated journey. It was the first chance I had to go abroad on a significant trip alone, without the security blanket of a family or friends. I had flights booked, but the rest was a blank itinerary – my aim had been to fill it with a successful ascent. I had sourced the logistics, the food, a guide, accommodation and, with much relief, made the top on my 19th birthday. In an imperfect, and far from recommended, way I had successfully climbed the second mountain in my Seven Summits quest and it gave me the belief and confidence to further pursue this goal.

4

———

A Dangerous Obsession

To lose confidence in one's body is to lose confidence in oneself.

Simone de Beauvoir

Teenagers obsess about and battle against insecurities. The intense vulnerability during this unique period in one's life leaves young males and females comparing themselves unfavourably with unattainable levels of perfection accentuated by social media and the filtered visions people share of their lives. Despite a secure upbringing, I was also just another teenager with an emotional imbalance trying to understand myself better.

My school was high achieving. From our first day we were told, both directly and indirectly, that the barriers to success were there to be knocked down. Striving for excellence was not something to be embarrassed about. Setting ambitious goals in any sphere was seen as a realistic and achievable path to follow. Despite many success stories, this ethos also had the potential to plant excessive seeds of self-doubt if one did not reach those standards. Although there was a mentality of maximum involvement in different activities in order to seek the right path for you, it was hard not to compare oneself with others.

I believe humans, especially at that impressionable age, are hugely susceptible to outside influences. The British philosopher, Alan Watts, said, 'A lot of the current quest for identity among younger people is a search for an acceptable image.' There is a reason people start smoking, take up drugs or turn to alcohol in their teenage years. All those stimulants serve to create a sense of belonging, of being different, and of being more mature.

I was good at sport but not the best. I was intelligent but not the brightest. I met girls and ticked the key boxes of male adolescence, namely by losing my virginity earlier than many, but I never felt truly comfortable or sociable compared with others. I was a sheep rather than a shepherd. I started to smoke and it gave me a sense of freedom. The risk of buying alcohol and cigarettes underage with fake ID was all part of creating a façade of social normality. I had a reasonable cohort of friends but still craved approval from other groups that seemed to possess a stronger bond. In hindsight, I was probably like many other teenagers battling to ascertain their own identity. I believe that even the seemingly cocksure guys in my year had similar thoughts, but they were masked behind a veneer of bravado and showmanship.

I can look back at photos of myself as a slightly awkward teenager and am amused at the ill-fitting clothing, the dodgy glasses and the body yet to grow into adulthood. Beneath the surface, though, is something that troubled me more, and was probably a reason why my subconscious sought an outlet elsewhere.

According to the NHS, an eating disorder is 'characterised by an abnormal attitude towards food that causes someone to change their eating habits and behaviour. A person with an eating disorder may focus excessively on their weight and shape, leading them to make unhealthy choices about food with damaging results to their health.'

As of 2018, approximately 1.5 million people in the UK have an eating disorder. The statistics for teenagers, transitioning through a period of intense vulnerability and insecurity, stack up alarmingly. Ninety-five percent of those who suffer from eating disorders are between the ages of 12 and 25 while 11 percent of all those affected are male. I suffered from anorexia nervosa, I suffered from binge eating disorder (BED) and I suffered from bulimia. All of which are dangerous mental health problems that affect individuals physically, psychologically and socially.

Eating disorders are complex and often without a sole cause. They are linked to a combination of factors including stress, personal relationships, family breakups, obsessive personalities and psychological problems. Often the demands of sporting prowess in, for example, cycling, athletics, horse riding and gymnastics require extreme weight loss to achieve success and the pressure from coaches can amplify that. Every person with an eating disorder, however, has an individual story. They go through their own personal struggle before either fighting it, or letting it formulate the narrative.

Not long before reading *Facing Up*, I was starting to battle my own demons. Anxieties which would, in one form or another, stay with me for a number of years; arguably persisting even today in a different guise. I accepted this as an issue a long time ago but discussed it with very few people indeed. I now believe strongly in making people aware in order to combat the potentially deadly effects it can have. It is possible to overcome this problem and it is possible to live a normal life beyond the compulsive focus on food and weight.

I was always a decent runner but had stagnated after injuries. I decided to take it up again aged around 16 – not seriously but as a way to get fitter and faster. The explanation of how eating disorders develop and the mindset of the person concerned are sometimes hard to comprehend. What began as a small step back into fitness quickly developed into body dysmorphic disorder (BDD). BDD does not, as many mistakenly think, represent vanity but is rather a constant and relentless worrying about the flaws in one's appearance. I became obsessed with my body fat and current weight. I believed, as is extremely common for those with eating disorders, that by achieving the goals I had set myself in terms of my physical appearance, everything else in my life would fall seamlessly into place.

At the age of 17, I ran and ran; whenever I could really. Not fast and not far but it was the start of an obsession. Both the climbing journey and my eating disorder were inexorably linked in the desire to achieve a certain goal.

I began to run further and faster as my body weight dropped. Yet, cruelly, a wheel of disenchantment and dissatisfaction had started rolling. Eating disorders are uncompromising in their consumption of one's mental and physical reserves. They are dangerous because there is no halfway house, or at least there was not with me. The disorder demands constant attention, leading to constant anxiety. It plagues one's thoughts throughout the day, with both anticipation of what lies ahead and guilt about what has happened before. It generates a fear of food, a fear of one's own fallibility and a fear of social shaming.

I did not eat properly after extreme amounts of exercise, in the knowledge that doing so would undermine the weight loss focus of my regime. I meticulously counted calories for everything I consumed. I would deliberately skip meals and take pride in getting further through the day without touching food. My dopamine fix was seeing the clock reach a new hour in the day where I had lasted before eating.

Bulimia is the worst and most observable eating disorder. It is painful to think about and unpleasant to do. It is impossible to find joy or satisfaction in making yourself throw up. It provokes only feelings of guilt and shame.

Having starved my body of calories, my mind would yield to temptation, and I would find myself gorging on an excessive amount of food in a short space of time. It did not matter what it was, but it always happened when nobody else was around and there would be no evidence. The guilt then took over and the only way to find solace was to throw it up again and thus remove the possibility of any calorific gain. Catching sight of the pained expression on my face and tearful eyes in the mirror, as I sought to lubricate my coarse throat with water, after draining it of phlegm and bile, only amplified the guilt.

What is concerning was how regular and functional bulimia became. My body genuinely adapted to the strains I was putting it through. At most meals I would seemingly eat a normal portion – positive social perception and secrecy were key – before discreetly going to the bathroom and purging. I would clean the toilet, wash my hands, brush my teeth and then often have a cigarette to mask the smell on my breath. It was my own efficient little routine. My obses-sion was allowed to continue with nobody the wiser.

It is sad to think about now. I am fortunate in the family and friends I have who would never have judged me. Who, even as I write this now, remain ignorant of the extent of my struggle. I know that reading this will sadden them, but it shouldn't. I did everything I could to keep this my secret. I did not want anyone to know. This sort of behaviour was so unexpected in a male teenager that, any time I was almost caught, I would blame it on an illness or food poisoning. People with eating disorders are only too aware of their faulty character so keeping it under wraps was essential to maintaining the disguise of a normal life.

The love of my family is absolute but I closed them off,

along with everyone else, and just accepted this new form of normality. They supported me in my Seven Summits endeavour, but I was extremely good at hiding what was going on beneath the surface.

Becky Henry wrote the book *Just Tell Her to Stop*, which outlines the lack of understanding of these issues. It is not a question of telling someone that they aren't fat. I could look at a BMI index or get a set of callipers out and judge my body fat percentage to prove that I was not scientifically overweight. That would not have changed what my deluded brain said; it said I was. The challenge, rather, lies in getting people to believe in themselves, to have a genuine understanding of who they are and that they're valued.

I don't know the answer to the question of whether it is possible to fully recover from an eating disorder. I have had an emotional, conflicting and sometimes unpleasant relationship with food for over a decade. I do not suffer from bulimia anymore, and I am grateful for that. I am more understanding of my physical makeup, and of who I am, both physically and emotionally. It does not mean I eat what I want, when I want. I try to live a fairly healthy life. I eat the right stuff and enjoy exercise for the simple pleasure it brings of being in nature and sharing experiences. If that means I am recovered then, yes, I am. Given the psychological conflict that I experienced for many years, I can say that with pride and relief.

Why these things emerge in different people I will never know, but humans are flawed and vulnerable. I was, despite a loving upbringing, flawed and vulnerable. I stumbled upon my own path as a means to combat this shortcoming, and then attempted to turn it into something meaningful. Climbing Aconcagua and Kilimanjaro, although not eradicating the issue by any stretch, were some of the smaller steps I took towards the real end goal: inner contentment.

Elbrus

5,642m / 18,510ft

If adventure has a final and all-embracing motive, it is surely this: we go out because it is our nature to go out...

Wilfrid Noyce

I had adapted to the routine of taking a few days off after returning from a trip before locating my steel-toe-capped boots, my tool belt, electrical tape and cable ties and heading back to the world of marquees. It was my main income source, combined with catering at weekends. My passion for the work was limited but my desire to earn enough money for my next expedition to Russia was substantial. My social life consisted of living vicariously through the people I worked with, who headed off at week-ends to parties in London, to get pissed and get laid. I would be at home researching kit, reading epic mountaineering tales and focusing on the things within my control to enable these expeditions to get off the ground.

I climbed with a British company, Adventure Peaks, for Aconcagua. I emailed Dave when the Seven Summits idea came to my head and he probably thought, 'Here we go again' as another wistful youngster longs to stand at the highest point on earth. After my successes on Aconcagua, where I was one of the youngest Brits to stand on its summit, and Kilimanjaro, they probably knew that I had determination on the mountains but needed to match that with motivation and focus throughout my life. That is often what determines whether such ambitions result in success or failure.

After getting the Seven Summits idea in my head, Jake was one of the first people I emailed, another Brit who had climbed Everest a few years before. I asked him about acclimatising, kit and training – the usual requirements that often slot into place happily as one's experience builds. He told me, 'Strength of mind is more important than strength of leg.' I understood the mantra but, for me, the two are intrinsically linked.

I have always been athletically fit, so going running, hiking or cycling was part of my nature. For me, the knowledge that this was training for the mountains gave me even greater strength. I knew that when I pushed it a little bit harder on a run to make my lungs burn or went out on the bike when the rain was lashing it down and the roads slippery I was setting myself apart from other people. I wanted to be that guy who was so absorbed by a goal that it would overpower all other facets of life.

I remember watching *Sports Personality of the Year* and a friend said, 'This is a silly award, obsessive sports people have no personality.' I was fast becoming a guy without a personality. I was so driven by this objective that it was taking over. It was to dominate my finances, my food choices and my social life but I was blinkered in my perspective and under the impression that this was all that mattered.

After a number of months in this monotonous but necessary routine, I had accumulated enough funds to cover the trip. I visited Steve's shop in Ringwood again to keep him posted on my plans and seek reassurance I was making the right move. My kit stock was in a reasonable place, the conditions and requirements for Elbrus being similar to Aconcagua, but speaking to him was always informative.

The day before our departure, 8 August 2008, I got a call from Stu at Adventure Peaks to confirm the expedition was still going ahead. He had spoken to his contacts in the area and it was stable enough to proceed. I was blissfully unaware of world politics. He told me to read the news – what is now known as the Russo-Georgian War had just kicked off as Russian separatists sought to exert their control and influence over the region. Heavy artillery shelling was underway in Abkhazia in what was regarded as the first European war of the 21st Century.

Elbrus in Russia, standing at 5,642m, or 18,510ft, is the highest mountain in Europe. Popular wisdom would wrongly have it to be Mont Blanc (4,808m/15,774ft) in the French Alps – the highest in Western Europe. The Caucasus mountain range, together with the Ural Mountains further north, is historically representative of the border between Europe and Asia. Elbrus, being on the northern edge of the

Caucasus Mountains in southern Russia, therefore fits just within the Europe boundary.

I bid Mum farewell before meeting my new teammates and starting another adventure. Looking back now, I realise I was extremely selfish in my activities over this period and relied heavily on the flexibility and compliance of my parents. I was living with them and choosing a path they knew was contrary to the norm. With the benefit of age and wisdom on their side, they allowed me to go away and undertake these challenges with minimal input. In some ways, I had closed people out of the loop but selectively opened up about the plan I had in place and my parents were always supportive. On a subconscious level, this had an enormous impact on what I was trying to achieve.

Without the support and belief of those close to you, achieving any significant goal throws out challenges that can be insurmountable. Just as I was never pushed into this challenge, I was never encouraged by my parents to give it up when it appeared a lost cause. Instead, I was given the self-belief that it was possible. My dad is a huge admirer of entrepreneurs who belligerently pursue their dreams when others do not have the foresight to comprehend it. Steve Jobs once said, 'You cannot connect the dots looking forward; you can only connect them looking backward. So you have to trust that the dots will somehow connect in your future.'

I could not foresee the journey ahead of me. I could, however, embrace the moment I was living in and take advantage of this drive that consumed my being, hoping that the dots would connect.

When I went for a pee at Heathrow, above the urinal was a news article from page three of *The Times*. There was a graphic of an explosion in southern Russia, on the Georgian border, and various facts and figures about the conflict that was taking place. I remained in place for what probably appeared an awkwardly long time – thankfully there wasn't a queue – and took it all in. Despite limited geographical knowledge of the area, I knew Elbrus lay somewhere within that explosion symbol. The conflict, according to the UK media, was engulfing the region in political and logistical turmoil; the Foreign Office advised against travel to the area. I wandered back to my teammates and, if nothing else, we had a starting point for conversation and a mutual wariness and excitement about where we were heading.

The team covered a wide spectrum of ages, backgrounds, experiences and motivations. Seemingly the only thing we had in common was our goal to climb Elbrus. Being thrown together with a variety of people and then living and climbing together is part of the overall experience. The first few hours of meeting each other on this type of trip provide fascinating insights into human psychology.

Unlike on Aconcagua, I was not the youngest and nor was I the least experienced. People seemed impressed I had climbed Aconcagua and Kilimanjaro so young and my high-altitude experience was above that of others. Instead of being wide-eyed and ignorant, constantly sponging off others, I found myself being asked questions. I was not seen as the 'one to watch' due to my inexperience but rather as someone who could help others. I felt a bit of a fraud in this regard and still told white lies about how much Scottish winter climbing I had done outside those expeditions. Despite my growing confidence with altitude and fitness, I knew there would be unforeseen challenges ahead.

We met our guide, Dmitry. Effervescent, extrovert and self-confident, he was as hilarious as he was vain. Dmitry was the guy who would perch himself on a rock 20m away from the group with a gorgeous backdrop. He would proceed to take his shirt off, in conditions that in no way warranted such action, and light up a cigarette with the full knowledge that he would be making it into photo albums and anecdotes in households across the UK. Unsurprisingly his body fat percent was negligible, his long blonde hair and sharp features were clearly Russian and he was not someone you would challenge in hand-to-hand combat. With him in charge, we felt content with our chances against the obstacles on the mountain – and any oncoming Georgian forces.

We stayed several nights in an architecturally questionable building with scaffolding erratically laddered across its frontage. A fluid number of workers dared to pioneer their way across to the next section and we watched in mild awe and surprise. Dmitry assured us this was standard Russian building maintenance protocol, the risk of collapse was minimal and we Westerners were too risk averse. With a life seemingly on the brink of another daring venture or ski-touring escapade, he was probably within his rights to say so, but it hardly did much to ease our concerns.

We acclimatised on routes nearby, honed some of our mountaineering skills on steep ice faces and enjoyed the freedom of being away from the UK and the trivialities of working life. We learned of each other's previous mountaineering exploits and exchanged stories about the trials and tribulations of being at the mercy of local guides and perilous conditions. Our British guide, Chris, was another outgoing and likeable character, as well as a very knowledgeable climber, who worked well developing each of us and bringing the team together. I had a passionate group of Yorkshiremen alongside me – not for the first or last time on climbing trips – and I began to understand more about the technicalities and joys of climbing in the UK.

With my limited experience, I admired the great climbers who pioneered new routes, who ventured into the unknown, encountered great loss but achieved huge success: the biggest and most darling exploits on notable mountains. However, gradually I started to realise that often the smaller and less celebrated pursuits bring the greatest joy. That could be taking children up their first Munro, long hikes with a loved one or turning around in a blizzard on the Pyg trail on Snowdon – these are the times that generate memories and kindle interest in other ventures.

We acclimatised near Krumrichi (4,200m) amid rocky and sparsely inhabited surroundings. This assisted our bodies to develop the red blood cells required for higher up. We caught a glimpse of Elbrus from afar with its distinctive dual summits, both dormant volcanic domes. They differ in height by a mere 21m and their snow-capped hats were the noticeable feature on the landscape. At the base of Krumrichi we joined a party of Russian climbers who had travelled from near Irkutsk, almost 5,000km away. To me, Irkutsk represented nothing but a territory to be ransacked on the board game Risk. Hearing stories of this team and their perilous and complex journey just to get to the Caucasus Mountains was remarkable. Half a village of over 80 people had decided to come on this pilgrimage to attempt climbing the highest mountain in their beloved country. Unsurprisingly, Dmitry was fully committed to this impromptu Russian party, and started to drain their supply of vodka at a rate that would terminate most men.

I felt optimistic about the climb ahead and believed my competence at altitude and personal resilience would stand me in good stead. By physically removing myself from my insular working routine, I was trying to manage my issues with food. A new group of teammates who respected me was a positive influence in how I was to try to combat this unpleasant eating disorder.

A couple of days' rest ensued before we moved upwards to the barrel huts at the base of Elbrus. It was shelter from the elements and would allow us to prepare our kit before a few more acclimatisation hikes and then our attempt on the summit. Days like this provide a genuine opportunity to relax, reflect and just be. There were no time pressures and no distractions, so we could read, exchange stories and play cards. With Michael, also aged 19, I settled into games of chess and compared whose facial hair growth was the more embarrassing. It was good to have another young guy around with whom I could relate.

Dmitry recounted tales of the early attempts on Elbrus when we were at the barrel huts. The first recorded ascent of the east summit, 21m lower, was in 1829 by the Russian, Khillar Khachirov. For unknown reasons, there then appears to have been a 45-year gap before the first ascent of the west summit by a British expedition in 1874. Why Khillar did not think, 'Just to cover my bases I might pop up the west summit as well', is baffling to me, as is the fact that nobody else in the next half-century tried either. Regardless, the opportunistic Brits, led by F. Crauford Grove, had no reservations and ploughed on to the true summit, much to the dismay of the Russians. We enjoyed reminding Dmitry of this little fact, but we also said that if he could take the left-hand fork instead of the right-hand one, it would be much appreciated. I would not have put it past him to lead a team of Brits to the east summit just for his own amusement.

We stepped out of the hut in the dark and the bitter cold struck me. Venturing out from our shelter into the elements was something I had not become truly accustomed to yet, but I was excited to grip my crampons into the snow and move up. The temperature dip ensured keeping our extremities warm was a struggle for the opening gambit. The old adage, 'Be bold, start cold', is psychologically tough to start with but came to fruition as our bodies adapted and our bobbing cones of light meandered up the slopes. As climbs go, it was not technical nor was it particularly steep but, as the winds picked up, visibility dropped to almost nothing and the swirling snow stunted progress. Dmitry led the way.

Rarely are long climbs or long days in the mountains enjoyable throughout. As when going for a lengthy run, when one starts there is initial enthusiasm as energy levels are high, and that can transcend into a more peaceful phase. This is why I run, cycle, cross-country ski and climb – because it is in that phase that the nature around you appears more vivid, the colours jump out and the sounds seep deep into your brain. There is always a dip when enthusiasm wanes a bit, when you realise you're actually having to work a bit harder and the end goal is not immediately in sight. This is the phase where the mind has to work to convince itself that the end will come and the pain will cease. This is the phase when *sisu* becomes such a key element of expeditions. *Sisu* is about getting your brain to maintain that commitment and forward momentum. When one moves as a team, even more so when you are roped together, you are restricted to the speed and the momentum of the slowest person. Everyone has doubts and distractions that creep into their minds, but the key is to just keep moving, stay with the person in front and try to distract the mind from the discomfort the body may be in.

It took us over six hours to zigzag our way towards the summit slopes. The limited visibility and strong winds reduced our overall speed despite the moderate gradients. The team maintained reasonable morale but we each endured an insular climbing rhythm in the conditions. When we finally made it to the top, instead of being basked in sunshine and clear blue skies with a resplendent Russian view beneath us, we could see no further than a couple of metres due to the fog and falling snow. Of the three expeditions I had been on that year, two of them had resulted in a negligible view at the top. After a few photos, none of us was in the mood for hanging about and we headed off back down the mountain. In terms of a triumphant summit, it was an anticlimax, but given the situation, it was just a relief to make the top. Nature, sadly, does not yield to the wishes of a hopeful mountaineer.

Unlike on Aconcagua, I had managed my efforts in a much

more mature fashion, fuelled correctly and felt strong. I felt confident in my own strength to undertake a reasonably demanding trip and remain in good shape. I had not built up a layer of intrigue and fear around Elbrus in the way I had with Aconcagua. Put crudely, I wanted to ensure I made it to the top to complete the first phase of this project before I started at university a month later.

The next hour of going downhill was a major challenge for some. Two guys began to struggle with the altitude and exhaustion. I think Michael's state was similar to mine on Aconcagua; after achieving his major milestone, one which he'd had doubts he could achieve beforehand, he started to falter. I followed him step by step for the majority of the descent until the conditions cleared up. He was never going to be in any serious drama – the conditions and his reasonable physical state would not allow that to happen – but it added an element of difficulty. When we reached the wider slopes, Dmitry took over, attaching a short rope and a karabiner to him. They descended with Michael sliding down the mountain on his ass and the Russian halting his downward momentum with crampons gripping into the fresh snow. It was another illustration of the power of mountains and the resourcefulness they demand and of how, even when things are going smoothly, a situation can turn in an instant.

The post-climb antics again provided a heightened layer of intrigue. Moving on from an assault and police line-up in Argentina to financial insolvency and sleeping rough in Kenya, I thought I'd keep my head below the parapet in war-torn Russia. The sun was shining, the climbing phase of the expedition was complete and three of us decided to go for a wander along the riverbed and explore the area. Admittedly we should have taken heed of the large blue sign that read:

ATTENTION!
ZONE OF THE BORDER CONTROL!
PASSES AND DOCUMENTS ONLY

However, we sauntered on admiring the waterfalls and planning out imaginary climbing routes on nearby cliff faces. Next thing we knew, a trio of Russian Army uniforms were charging towards us from all directions. Where the hell did they come from and what was our plan of action? Fight, flight or freeze. Fighting appeared an unwise choice as AK-47s were being aimed at us. Flight was probably not recommended due to the aforementioned weapons so we froze, hands in the air, awaiting our fate. Russian-British translation was non-existent but gestures indicated exactly what was required. Tails between our legs, but slightly relieved and amused, we headed back to the structurally questionable hotel and recounted what had happened. Needless to say, Dmitry found the whole thing hilarious. It added fuel to his developing sense of Western weakness. He explained that had we continued along our pleasant mountain path we would have soon entered Georgia. Given the political disturbance, I can understand why the border guards acted in the way they did.

It had been a successful trip and Elbrus represented the third and final mountain before starting at St Andrews. Dreaming up a big challenge is the easy bit. Taking the necessary steps to make it happen is when the challenge becomes more demanding and is the test of one's commitment.

In an eight-month period, I had succeeded in standing at the highest points in Europe, Africa and South America – all self-funded and self-motivated. I had set aside the year to make inroads into this dream and thankfully it had been a success. What if I had not made the summit of Aconcagua? What if, after all that research and dreaming, I had fallen at the first hurdle? As it transpired, the mountain gods were looking kindly on me and allowed me a 100 percent success rate. I knew future tests were to be encountered but at that moment I was fully committed to the task at hand in the knowledge that taking the first few steps of the journey are often the hardest.

6

DISTRACTION

But whether explorer or not, I have one advice to give you: stick to the work you begin in life, till the task is finished and finished well, whatever it may be. Go into it with your whole heart and your whole mind.

Fridtjof Nansen

After Elbrus, my mind was transfixed by the Seven Summits and what lay next. Attending my sister's birthday party the day after I returned, I explained to people my reluctance to go to university when I had another plan in place. The idea of attending lectures and focusing on academia again after over a year of dedication to a totally different kind of pursuit seemed unappealing.

Those sentiments are probably shared by almost everyone who has been away for a gap year. How simple life appears when immersed in another plan or another country. There was a feeling of dread of returning to normality, to the real world, to the inescapable pursuit of employment and pragmatism. I felt a genuine urge to flee that conveyor belt, continue to earn money doing whatever job helped me make enough to continue my project. It had no specific deadline but I knew if I remained focused then it was possible.

Neither my parents nor my sisters, both students at the time, told me to get a grip or get over myself. They did, however, convince me to head to Scotland and at least try to embrace the first few weeks before making a decision. I decided to set the Seven Summits to one side for the time being and just be a student.

Within a matter of days of being at St Andrews, I felt I had found somewhere that just felt right. The university is a unique place situated on the east coast of Scotland about an hour north of Edinburgh. It has under 8,000 students compared with, for example, 23,000 at Oxford or 33,000 at Edinburgh. It is small, quirky, isolated, has one fairly questionable club and is surrounded by seven golf courses. I had made the choice to go there for precisely those reasons, same as my dad, and probably the same as my grandmother before him. It attracts a certain type of person who is probably not yearning for big city life and is instead seeking another kind of fulfilment in the distinctive makeup of the third oldest university in the English-speaking world.

Despite it being one of the top five universities in the UK, I'd been one of very few in my year at school to apply to St Andrews. As highlighted by the previous year's escapades, I wanted to forge my own path away from the masses. And I was rejected when I first applied. Never one to take no for an answer, I wrote a letter. Seeing as that did not get the response I was after, I then wrote another and offered to meet with the admissions team the following day, and then changed the subject for which I was applying. Thankfully, they got the hint. All of these things happen for a reason, and it probably says a lot about my character that I pursued it so doggedly, but it was finally up to the Auld Grey Toon it was.

My family did not hear from me for a number of days and assumed that 'No news is good news' and I must be having a good time. They were correct. The first four months until Christmas went by in a blur, literally as well as figuratively. My Seven Summits ambitions, which had been my sole focus, suddenly took a back seat. The distractions were obvious: alcohol, women, new friends and, of course, attending a few lectures. It was all an amazing set of experiences to immerse myself in. I embraced where I was, I loved it there and took pride in being a student.

When discussing gap years with fellow students, I knew mine was different but I never really let people into the wider plan. I made light of what I had achieved, which I had begun to realise was odd in comparison with most. That is not to say it was better or worse; I genuinely think that people find stimulation from different things. It was, however, different and had involved sacrificing so much time and effort. I had become a better version of myself. Some of the insecurities were still there and, like anyone in such a situation, I probably craved acceptance and recognition of who I was as a person rather than as a climber.

Having avoided a significant social life for the majority of the previous year, it felt special to be amongst so many like-minded people at a similar stage in life. I made friends who I knew would stay with me for years to come. I fell in love and had my heart broken. I got drunk and made a fool of myself. I smoked fervently and for a time lived the hedonistic and carefree life that I had previously suppressed. In many ways it was a delight to be on the normal path again, to take the well-trodden route, and just be young, make mistakes and not be judged for them. It was enlightening to be free from the shackles I had placed on myself in the previous year in terms of lifestyle and finance. I could just be a student at what I viewed as the best university in the world.

Through social acceptance, trust and understanding of what I had achieved, I was beginning to win the fight against bulimia. It is a vicious disorder that eats away at one's conscience and confidence. It attacks one's vulnerabilities and preys on all the insecurities that surround teenagers in particular. Social acceptance and self-awareness were key elements to me in battling that problem.

I began the Seven Summits journey not because I was bulimic and unable to eat a substantial meal without feeling an overwhelming sense of guilt and throwing it up alone in a bathroom. Rather I climbed because it gave me purpose. It gave me an avenue to express a part of my soul that had been craving to explore. Climbing liberated the part of my character that wanted to be different. It wanted uniqueness, stories to tell and pictures to show. That is what I believe combatting eating disorders is about: finding self-worth and purpose away from the restrictions you have imposed and allowing yourself to be free.

I had true friends who trusted me and would look out for me. They were the friends who would be there for me over the coming years when I needed them most. They were the friends who allowed me to be me and, without their knowledge, allowed me to begin the journey to overcome this all-encompassing issue.

Bear Grylls wrote in *Facing Up*, 'True commitment is following through with something long after the mood you said it in has passed.' For four months I allowed my Seven Summits plans to unravel. My priorities had shifted and the distractions of university life had taken centre stage. I rarely went running, rarely spent time researching or reading about climbing, and was not saving the money I required. Most people's grand plans for adventure often collapse at this stage. Choosing the untrodden path, when the main one is clearly more fun, is not easy.

Sometimes one can get a spark of inspiration from somewhere unexpected. A friend was competing in the BBC show *Last Man Standing*. I looked up to Ed and one of the challenges was to go to Nepal and race up a 4,000m mountain. He won the contest not through raw pace or brute strength but rather through perseverance and a willingness to endure: through *sisu*. I watched him collapse at the top and felt inspired and emotional because I knew what I needed to do. I went straight onto the Adventure Peaks website and paid the deposit to climb Denali the following summer. It was over seven months away but I knew that once that deposit had been paid, my mind would commit, and I would do my best to make it happen.

A switch flicked almost immediately in my head and rather than embracing the here and now, I was fast forwarding ahead to the summer and how I was going to tackle this severe mountain. Denali, in Alaska, was a noticeable step up and, from my research, I gathered that it would be physically demanding, logistically tough and involve intimidating costs. I remember taking a few bets with mates that I would not smoke from New Year's Eve until returning from Alaska. They had known me a matter of months, and that period had been spent predominately in a blur of alcohol and cigarettes, so from their perspective it appeared an easy win. I knew, however, that when 2009 came around, cigarettes would be so far down the priority list as to not even be a consideration. It was a no-brainer for me.

This change of mentality comes at a price and some people struggled with the change. My girlfriend, Kate, was my first love, intelligent, adoring, and energetic. We had a very intense few months and grew close, closer than I had been with anyone before. However, falling in love with someone in your first year at university can be a bit of a rollercoaster. And falling in love with a sociable and relaxed individual is different from going out with someone who is an individualist and focused. I think Kate understandably struggled with this transition. Suddenly, instead of attending things together in the evenings, I would stay back, save money and prepare for training the next day. This was not the person Kate had fallen for. Tension built in our relationship and, instead of fighting for it, we began to drift apart. I was not willing to sacrifice my attempt on Denali and she was not willing to sacrifice her lifestyle; something had to give.

I got my heart broken by Kate as she ended up falling for someone else. Emotionally I was fractured, but with the support of friends and family and, crucially, a clear objective to aim towards, it was far less obtrusive than it could have been. One of my best mates, Jonny, a wonderfully kind and foresighted individual, took me for a run and we reflected on the situation.

'The thing is, Stew, life is shit sometimes. It just throws crap at you and somehow we just have to proceed. Use those feelings you have now as motivation. When training is tough, when it gets shitty on that mountain, think of the anguish you feel now and it'll motivate you forwards.' He was right, of course, and we celebrated by doing our ritual pier jump into the North Sea.

A new mountain meant new requirements in terms of training. I needed to be physically stronger for the next stage as it would require pulling sleds and carrying heavy loads in variable conditions. Simply running and building my cardiovascular fitness was not enough anymore. Being based at St Andrews enabled me to train in the sand dunes, and I ventured to the west coast and made ascents of Ben Nevis and other Munros in the area.

On one notable occasion, seven of us headed to a hostel and planned to tackle the tourist route on Ben Nevis. I had done this plenty of times and knew the route well but was aware, despite what the others believed, that Scottish winter weather could be treacherous. Two of the six, Brendan and Duncan, were charming and erudite east coast Americans, who had been in the UK only a matter of months. The forecast did not fill me with much enthusiasm but, with Ranald and I as fairly experienced mountain men, the team was content to proceed up.

Lulled into a false sense of security on the lower slopes, our morale was high, food blissfully passed around and progress smooth. Suddenly, about two-thirds of the way up, as is the tendency in Scotland, the conditions turned. The glistening winter sun had been shocked into submission. The previously gentle breeze had taken steroids, while the horizontal hail assaulted the bare flesh on our cheeks. It was quite a shock but, being macho young men, nobody really expressed their true sentiments except in thinly veiled tongue-in-cheek shouts over the wind such as, 'Well this is unexpected,' and 'Nobody wanted it to be easy.' Despite everyone having a bleak time, we all just put our heads down, followed the feet in front and refused to be the guy who said enough was enough.

I could see what was happening, went to the front, spoke to Ranald and offered everyone the get-out-of-jail-free card we all secretly craved. They knew I was enough of a masochist to willingly crack on but instead, I asked, 'Seriously, guys, who actually wants to continue on? We can all acknowledge this is fairly shit.' One sheepish hand went up and its owner said, 'Well, I wouldn't mind actually, I can barely feel my fingers.' Then everyone quickly joined in with, 'I haven't felt my toes for about half an hour so it might be best,' and, 'Yep, this is truly crap. Let's get a beer.' We made it down, found a bar, settled in with pints all round and began to wage war on the real battlefield of human emotion – the board game Risk.

Ben Nevis offered another small insight into the uncontrollable nature of mountains. They can turn in an instant from appearing friendly and convivial to being inhospitable and malicious. Mountains demand determination and fortitude from us, as well as humility and respect. Climbing mountains is aspirational, in that people see scaling them as a barometer of achievement. Each climber knows they are at the mercy of nature and only the mountain decides whether you climb or not.

To prepare for the sled-pulling requirements of Denali, I browsed around on eBay and found a small wooden sled on sale from a guy in the Midlands. This little sled would provide a key component to my training, functionally but also helping to make this solo venture more inclusive. I rigged up my harness to the front of the sled and got female friends to sit on the back while I dragged them up and down West Sands beach in St Andrews. For them this entailed the relatively simple task of staying still, putting on a set of headphones and enjoying the view of town as I toiled away up front. Unsurprisingly I got some very odd looks from locals who, however accustomed they were to erratic student behaviour, had probably not witnessed this sort of thing before. Slowly but surely I was building the physical robustness I would need for the expedition as well as the cardiovascular demands of coping in a harsh environment with limited oxygen.

7

Denali

6,190m / 20,310ft

The very basic core of a man's living spirit is his passion for adventure. The joy of life comes from our encounters with new experiences...

Christopher McCandless

In native Alaskan, the word Denali translates as the 'Great One' and with a larger bulk and higher rise than Everest, plus extremely erratic weather, it was an intimidating proposition. This was the first expedition I had gone on where friends had a genuine interest in, and understanding of, what I was undertaking. I kept the rest of the Seven Summits plan quiet from almost everyone but I suddenly had mates wishing me luck and following my progress; it was a change from the solitary nature of the previous year's experiences. Climbing the highest mountain in North America was a serious undertaking that people could relate to.

Preparations in the week before departure hardly filled me with optimism. I contracted severe tonsillitis and was in hospital on a drip for several days. My morale was being sapped by the day but thankfully it managed to heal; my concern about missing the trip subsided and I was home a few days before we were due to leave. The day before departure I woke and asked my sisters where Dad was. They informed me that my grandmother had passed away so he had driven to Scotland where she had lived. The news hit me hard and various scenarios went rushing through my head about the right thing to do while hoping Dad, an only child, was OK.

My grandmother had been a fiercely determined and intelligent woman whom I had respected hugely. I called Dad and asked him what I should do. He reassured me that I should go ahead with the expedition, not to worry about what was happening at home in terms of funerals and do the best I could in Alaska. He said my grandmother would have been proud of what I had achieved and of the endeavour I was about to undertake, which added a layer of motivation and pride to proceedings.

Back to Heathrow, more farewells and across the Atlantic we went. It appeared as though fate had it in for me when, after everything else that had happened in the last week, my luggage went missing, filled with the kit I would need for the next month. But meeting my new team was encouraging, as the level of competence and professionalism had increased again. I had huge respect for the people I would be relying on for the ensuing month.

The Alaskan Range stretches 400 miles across southcentral Alaska. It is a wild place, covered in glaciers and punctuated by rugged peaks. The crown of the range is Denali, at 6,190m the highest peak in North America. Located so close to the Arctic Circle, Denali can present some of the most challenging conditions of any mountain on earth. The weather can reach both ends of the spectrum, from calm sunlight to vicious Arctic winds, without warning. When we arrived at the park entrance, the statistics for the season were up and it had summit success rate at 55 percent. We looked at each other and wondered who would be in which half – but the statistic is not due to individuals, but rather whole teams who never get a chance due to the weather. It was out of our control so we concentrated on managing our own parameters and maximising our chances if the opportunity to summit presented itself.

Our team was multinational, covered a range of ages and immediately had a strong rapport. Our guide for the expedition was Heidi, a hugely experienced Colorado-based climber, whose enthusiasm and love for the outdoors was truly infectious. She lived for exploring, hiking and seeing individuals stretch their perceived comfort zones by taking on new endeavours in nature. I liked her from the start.

Scott, a teammate, was an accountant from London, something he was proud of, and he took pleasure in combating the accountant stereotype. Having summited Everest in 2006, he was looked up to for knowledge and expertise of high altitude. I badgered him with questions throughout, picking up titbits of information where I could. He was partnered for the expedition with Neil, a 22 year navy veteran, now working in London, who exuded confidence and enjoyment of life. They had climbed together before and consistently provided me with banter, amusement and support whenever it was required. Jaysen, a conscientious and highly motivated Mauritian actuary in London, completed the British contingent. Despite being the youngest again, I felt part of a strong team and less of an individual – something that would be crucial as the expedition developed.

A Twin Otter plane flew us from civilisation into the lower Kahiltna Glacier. It was like nowhere I had been before and I was struck by the grandeur and freedom that it offered. It was a beautiful and remote place that allowed one to escape the world and delight in its sheer glory at the same time. We erected our tents and spent our first night marvelling at the landscape that surrounded us. Many of us had reached greater altitudes before – Aconcagua is over 700m higher than Denali – but the latitude combined with the weather extremes ensured none of us could count our chickens.

Unlike on previous expeditions, teamwork was imperative to our success. From the first day until we flew off the ice, we would be roped together in three teams of four. The high crevasse risk along the glacier is such that if one person falls in, being tied to the others keeps them from going any further. This propagates a sense of trust among teammates as potentially you could be relied upon to fall on your ice axe and arrest the momentum of a fall. I enjoyed the cohesion that this required, rather than every person taking care of themselves.

Beyond the Brits, our team hailed from around the globe: the effervescent and highly successful Canadian businessman Shawn, a lovely Danish lady, Stina, and a Polish climber, Mirek, whose intimidatingly angular features and square jaw belied the kind heart within. Stina, Shawn and I were all planning to tackle Everest the following spring in our individual Seven Summits pursuits. Denali was, therefore, both an important step for building our mountaineering strength and key in keeping up momentum for our wider aim.

We had harnesses on from the beginning to drag sleds behind us, individual and team kit split between those and our rucksacks. The combined load was heavier than I had experienced, but thankfully my training stood me in reasonable stead and I felt fairly strong from the off. We had snowshoes on – increasing the surface area of one's footprint hugely reduces the chances of sinking every step. With snowshoes and the sled, it was a different feel to previous expeditions but I was a fan. I liked the freedom of travelling vast distances in the backcountry carrying everything you need. Like a snail with its home on its back, we were now reduced to a sled and rucksack to survive. Having so much kit required us to cache food and equipment higher up the mountain. We would hike up, use snow shovels to dig a suitably sized hole for what was needed and leave a flag to identify it before returning down. This process assisted with our acclimatisation and ensured we had suitable supplies for the higher slopes.

The key features of this part of the route included the notorious Heartbreak Hill, Motorcycle Hill and Windy Corner – all of which hardly generated hope. That is the joy of undertaking mountaineering expeditions in places one has read about. Some prefer to know little history of a mountain before climbing it, but I loved the literature including fabled tales of success, rescues and drama. Hearing descending teams talk of 'gnarly conditions at Windy Corner, man', when we asked how it was only added to the sense of excitement. I craved the challenge. I wanted to experience the demanding conditions and see how I would cope. Be careful what you wish for. Having safely established ourselves on a large glacial shelf known as Genet Basin, we could see more of the iconic features of the mountain including the Messner Couloir, the Orient Express, the Upper West Rib, Rescue Gully and the 200m ice slope named the Headwall. The names formulated fearsome images but the setting remained one of peace and harmony. The evening views with the sun not fully setting, painting the surrounding peaks in an orange-and-pink hue of alpenglow, stick in the mind.

I had read and seen the film adaptation of Jon Krakauer's *Into The Wild*, in which he recounts the tale of the intrepid traveller, Christopher McCandless, before he died in the Alaskan wilderness. I found McCandless a frustrating person in some ways; his selfishness in leaving his family without adequate reason and heading off into the sunset was beyond my comprehension. And yet equally, his free-spirited lust for life – for adventure, travel and human relationships – was inspiring. In his words, 'Nothing is more damaging to the adventurous spirit within a man than a secure future.' To his credit, he acted upon his instincts. I found his willingness to sacrifice those left behind too much to truly admire; but his act of heading into the foreboding and unforgiving wildness of Alaska was something that now resonated with me. The region is wild nature in its purest form.

Climbers on the mountain adopt the Norwegian approach to nature: 'Take only memories, leave only footprints,' thus allowing everyone their own opportunity to experience the calm and natural serenity. I can see why Chris McCandless had Denali on his list of things to accomplish whilst in Alaska – its remote and grand appeal is obvious. I can also see how its seductive yet compassionless landscape led to his demise.

On previous expeditions, our team would arrive at a campsite, pitch our individual tents and cook using a stove and freeze-dried meals. However the routine on Denali was different. Together we would dig a centralised eating space, about five feet down in the snow. Establishing the right size and angles for comfortable seating positions remained a dark art but, with practice, we began to perfect our style to accommodate all 12 climbers. Breakfast and evening meals were some of the highlights of the trip. Not because of the view – there were 12 of us in a small tent dug into the snow – but because it was there that cohesion and team bonding took centre stage. Huddled around a stove, physically tired, in down jackets in –30°C, there are none of the normal social boundaries of the outside world.

On expeditions, one's inhibitions are slowly withdrawn and that is a key reason why people bond so closely despite knowing each other for only a short amount of time. You see each other cold, tired, without makeup. Without the distractions and demands of the outside world, you are reduced to listening to each other's stories and perspectives on the world, which leads to a breadth of knowledge and reflection.

We loved hearing stories by Mirek, a former member of the Polish military, explaining what life was like in the Soviet Union – before he found his way to America, having fled the army. Annoyingly, this was something we never got to the bottom of; how he then ended up employed as a deep-sea diver, exploring shipwrecks, was equally bewildering. There was Neil, who signed up to the British Navy as a teenager and explored the world on six-month stints away from family and friends for over 20 years. There was Nick, a 28-year-old American pilot, and Seba, a Peruvian mountaineer – all giving raw insights into worlds I had not seen before. The variety and surprises in people's upbringing, motivations and endeavours could not fail to inspire and bring closeness in a group.

After a few days' rest, we made our first move up the Headwall to cache some clothing required for High Camp before proceeding the following day. The Headwall was steep but provided a good test of stamina and it was a relief that everyone made it successfully. The section from the top of the Headwall to High Camp included some of the more exciting parts of the climb. We navigated around rocky sections and clipped around snow pickets atop a sharp drop. Slowly the mountains that had loomed over us became wholly visible and only Mount Foraker, at 5,304m, appeared above our current altitude.

Upon reaching High Camp, we began to fortify our tents for the impending weather – the forecast was not ideal for the next few days. High Camp can be buffeted by extremely strong winds so we ventured out into the icy blasts with a snow saw and cut blocks to create a wall to protect the tents from the elements.

The fifth of July was a rest and acclimatisation day in our tents at 5,242m. There might have been a break in the weather but Heidi opted against going for it. I was ready, willing and felt strong but she wisely held us all back. The great British climber, Doug Scott, said, 'Nothing substitutes a large apprenticeship, a heap of experiences which converts into the base of intuition.' Heidi had the experience and knowledge of the mountain to keep us in place until a genuine window opened. Had the final result been different, I wonder how I would have felt about this decision, but her patience was steadfast. Heidi had a strong belief that 'climbing is about the journey, not the summit'. Although correct, it is easier to have that perspective when you have summited a number of times before and know you will get the chance again. For me, I felt this was my only shot, but we came as a team, with a guide, and therefore those decisions remained out of our hands.

Huge thunderheads moved through the range and passed by our tents, meaning everyone experienced an electrical charge. We were hoping it would leave us literally with our hair on end, but sadly nothing transpired. Regardless it was apparently quite a rare event on Denali. Another special natural beauty we experienced, and one that stands out for me, was an immensely vivid circular halo. This is produced by the light interacting with ice crystals in the atmosphere to form a circular ring of radiance around the sun.

The following day we spent sitting tight again; climbing sometimes requires seemingly limitless supplies of patience. The body might feel refreshed, the mind might be buzzing, but if the mountain says 'no' then the decision is made. The second day of being stuck at High Camp was frustrating but inescapable. Three of us cramped together in one tent with a makeshift washing line along our roof ensured that personal comfort and space was impossible. We had one-litre, wide-mouthed water bottles to pee in and anything more substantial was done in the porch – a good bonding experience certainly. These sorts of days are about waiting, refuelling and preparing for what is to come.

Expeditions allow freedom from modern-day distractions such as phones and social media, providing a rare opportunity to relax and guilt-free time to read that book that was given to you last Christmas or listen to that Bob Dylan album from start to finish – the way he designed it to be listened to. There was also a fear, however, that the brief weather window we'd had was gone and an opportunity had slipped through our fingers. There was a fear that we would have to descend due to lack of food and the whole team would miss the chance to summit. We were the last team on the mountain this season so there would be no second chance.

So when Heidi peered into our tent before we went to sleep and said we would be off at 7 a.m. the following morning, there was a huge sense of giddy excitement – not mad celebrations but relief that we would at least get a chance.

Suddenly, having been horizontal for 48 hours, each of us was on our knees trying to locate the bit of kit necessary for our summit attempt. We discussed contingency plans and each weighed up the merits of that extra Snickers bar or those extra mitts. A restless night ensued as our brains ticked over trying to think of what we might have forgotten. Equally, there was a buzz as finally the mountain had creaked opened its doors and permitted us to peek inside.

We woke and shook off the condensation from inside the tent – always a bracing way to start the day. We loaded our rucksacks, prepared our harnesses and split into our pre-designated rope teams. Heidi, Scott, Neil and I would take the lead, which suited me. I preferred being ahead, not for competitive reasons but because I felt more in control of my destiny. I found it gave a greater sense of freedom, rather than following in someone else's footsteps.

As we set out, there was a calmness, in stark contrast to the blustery and fitful weather we'd experienced over the previous 48 hours. This ensured our morale was high and there was an unspoken confidence among us that we could make it to the top without any dramas. Days like this on a mountain such as Denali are rare. We had struggled through some tough conditions and were forced to bide our time, but on this day the mountain gods were sympathetic.

We began by climbing the rising traverse known as the Autobahn, named after a pioneering German team, followed by Denali Pass, the saddle between the north and south summits, and then the Football Field, a broad plateau. There were some moderately steep snow climbs before the spectacular knife-edged ridge which runs to the summit came into view. We took a break and grabbed some water, confident that with all 12 of us there, the whole team would make it up. The summit ridge is quite something, with very significant drops either side and, as we climbed, I looked down at the whole south face which seemed to fall away over 2,000m to our left. Heidi, Scott, Neil and I dropped our ropes at a relatively flat spot and waited for the others. Together we took our final few steps to the summit of Denali, the highest mountain in North America.

With clear blue skies all around and negligible wind, it was a real pleasure to linger there with a wonderful team. Time was on our side so we could enjoy the view and take photos while reflecting on our good fortune. A passing sightseeing plane flew close and the passengers were greeted with 12 bare backsides as we celebrated our summit.

Video Diary – 8 July 2009

I'm at the top of North America, 6,190m and it's a hell of a feeling. The views are incredible. I just want to say thank you to everyone that has supported me or wished me luck, it means a lot.

I also want to say a word for my grandmother, who unfortunately I can't see when I get back down and I can't tell her stories of this trip, which she would have loved. But my thoughts are with her and I feel we have been well looked after by her because the guides, the weather and the team have all been amazing.

I feel truly blessed to be here today.

It was a wonderful moment but also emotional and I cried as I moved away from the group to reflect. I know my grand-mother would have been proud of what I had achieved. Her passing the day before I departed for Alaska had been at the forefront of my mind for much of the trip and served as extra motivation when it got challenging.

Despite our weariness, as we descended to High Camp we knew that what we had experienced was uncommon on such a wild mountain. The following day we headed down to Camp 1 and after overnighting there in sleeping bags and snow holes, inspired by Mirek and his Polish military days, we headed down again. Being the last team of the season made crossing the lower slopes of the mountain quite a daunting prospect as the melting snow made the crevasse risk extremely apparent. Poor Mirek was up front and our rope teams would regularly find him waist deep in snow that had given way underneath him. What began as unfortunate became hilarious as it continued happening. We assumed it was his poor route choice but it kept us (and thankfully him) entertained.

Within a few days we had made it back to the Twin Otter plane and were ready to fly back to civilisation. Leaving the Kahiltna Glacier and that Alaskan wilderness, I felt genuine sadness to be saying goodbye to such a special place. That was the first expedition where I felt genuine love for the natural surroundings. I saw the joy in the simplicity of just being in nature. The few nights of celebration that followed were indicative of the bond that our team had forged. I knew I would remember them and our attempt to climb Denali.

Heidi sent a message to Adventure Peaks after our return to the UK:

With a very fun, and very strong crew of climbers on the team, we got lucky with some excellent weather up there, as well as a team that stayed healthy throughout the entire climb. As I like to say, it is sometimes better to be lucky than good. What a great climb!!! Thanks to everyone on the team, Jaysen aka 'Veggie', Geordie, Neil, Scott; for all of their hard work on the climb, their willingness to work as a team, and for really sticking together, especially when it came to the late night celebrations of the last two nights in Anchorage!!!

Thanks to Geordie for his maturity in this case in particular, and at all other times as well. To Neil for keeping Geordie straight, to Scott for keeping him honest and finally to Jaysen for eating the chicken and bacon, even after I forgot to remove it from dinner, all with a smile on his face. May we all meet again climbing somewhere, sometime!!!

All the Best, Heidi

I quote that message for a number of reasons, but primarily because in spring 2010, Heidi Kloos, 41, died in an avalanche near her home in Colorado. She was highly experienced and not one to take unnecessary risks so it was a huge shock and immensely sad for the climbing community and her family.

Heidi was the best guide I have ever had. From our first encounter, we got on extremely well and I think she took a mentoring and maternal approach to me. I think she understood what I was seeking from this Seven Summits journey. Equally, she knew I loved being in that environment surrounded by like-minded people. She knew that I was too hasty to reach the summit and needed to learn the value of patience. She also knew when to stop, to look around and embrace the beauty of where we were. Beyond her excellent guiding ability, she was a hugely kind and enthusiastic person who extracted the best out of everyone. I feel sadness that she isn't around because, echoing what she said in her message to us, I would love to have climbed with her again somewhere, sometime. A great loss to the world.

8

Persistence is a Virtue

If it were easy, everybody would do it. But it's not. It takes patience, it takes commitment, and it comes with plenty of failure along the way.

Barack Obama

After the success of Denali, I had now reached the highest point in four of the seven continents, with Vinson, Carstensz Pyramid and Everest remaining to complete the challenge. I wanted to climb Everest in spring the following year before going to Indonesia for Carstensz and then to Antarctica to complete my Seven Summits by the end of 2010.

The previous mountain expeditions I could self-fund through hard work and sacrifice, but the requirements of the next three within my timeframe of only 18 months would require a different approach. My post-Alaska bank balance was negligible which left quite a daunting task in place. Ideally, one has a silent backer or a parent who can fund all expeditions, leaving training and getting up the mountain for the climber. In my early forays into mountaineering, I assumed that the climbing aspect was the toughest bit: the perseverance, skill and teamwork. I was to learn that just getting to the mountain was the real challenge, requiring exactly the same characteristics. The hard, and far less glamorous part, was about to begin.

I was back working at marquees after Denali and deliberating every day about the right path to take. *The next step had to be Everest, surely? But it's Everest, the highest mountain in the world. Are you really ready to climb Everest in nine months' time? Are you really willing to risk your life climbing Everest? Denali is one thing but Everest...* This was my ongoing internal dialogue until I called Adventure Peaks and paid my deposit to make an attempt from the north in 2010. I went to work the next day and told my colleagues that I was signed up for Everest the following year. My planned departure date was 3 April 2010 and it was in the diary. Suddenly, this had become a lot more real.

I decided to climb Everest in aid of the charity Help for Heroes. At this stage, I had no thoughts about joining the Army but I believed strongly in the charity. It had only been around for a couple of years but its aim of providing better facilities for British servicemen and women who had been wounded or injured in the line of duty was very compelling. The British Army deployments in Iraq and Afghanistan were regularly on the news and the selfless courage of these people warranted whatever support I could give. I knew the amount of money I raised would not be substantial; I was struggling even to get the funds to go on the expedition. However, if I were able to raise anything for Help for Heroes, as well as giving the charity more exposure, then it would provide further reason and motivation for my endeavours.

I was walking the dog one afternoon, one of my favourite times for reflection. I knew that the next part of this project would require assistance – beyond the support from friends, I would need someone to help manage the project and raise funds. Freddie was a good mate from St Andrews who had already made a name for himself in our first year for his event planning and unrivalled enthusiasm. He was extrovert but also intelligent, strategically able and creative. I would learn that above all these things he was immensely loyal and selflessly committed. He would soon become a trusted friend.

I called him, explained the current situation, and asked if he would lend a hand. Freddie, like me, can commit to things full steam if they trigger his interest. I can be idle and unproductive if I am not stimulated by something or lack true belief in a project, but will happily go into sixth gear if I do. Thankfully for me, he was on board, happy to be asked and immediately we had a planning day in the diary. Dad, Freddie and I spent a chaotic weekend brainstorming; it was a good start. Their strengths, especially Freddie's, lay in the ability to focus on what was required and the strategy to get there. Together we thought of creative ways to encourage people to sponsor me, inventive media angles and how best to maximise the brand.

'Nobody is going to pay for you to go on holiday, mate. Like it or not, you are going to have to market yourself or you'll never get there.' Freddie was brutally honest. 'Social media is how the world works now. If you don't want to do Twitter or Facebook, then either you won't get there or I'll do it for you. It's happening!'

This is how Freddie fed me the practical bits of advice I needed during a long afternoon playing Fifa on PlayStation. He was right: what had started as me going on a few expeditions had to escalate into something more if it was to have a successful conclusion. The first aspect was getting the idea out there across all channels and seeing what we could do to maximise exposure. We made a website, produced sponsorship proposals and tried to broker deals with newspapers and magazines, though our success was fairly limited. We debated whether to get lots of small sponsors for around £1,000, or focus solely on companies that might be willing to pay for the lot. I learned that to get sponsorship you need two things: firstly, a unique selling proposition (USP) to draw people in and, secondly, something that appeals to both the head and heart of a potential sponsor. Getting funds for Everest would be markedly easier than for the other two. Carstensz and Vinson together cost three times more than Everest but lacked the public recognition. Despite thinking long-term, we had to focus on the shorter term, which was getting the money for Everest.

While pursuing this project, we were still trying to complete our degrees and enjoy student life. The balance was a tough one to strike but I had a new girlfriend, Klara, who, like

Freddie, would be a key pillar supporting me over the next 18 months. We fell in love and she became a central part of my life. She was beautiful and intelligent, and would never fail to challenge my preconceptions. The passion and excitement of a new relationship turned out to be important as, around the same time, my parents had decided to split up after more than 25 years of marriage.

The disruption of family life added a new dimension to everything else that was going on and impacted my two sisters and I in different ways. I dealt with the situation in the best way I could, trying to understand the reasons and use rationality as the key tool to move forwards. Being in a small town on the Scottish coast, I was physically removed from the family home in the south of England. Emotionally I could not let myself be distracted, or the dream I had worked so hard to achieve for several years would have gone to waste.

I began to train hard again. I would head to the Highlands on a regular basis. Leaving on Friday to stay at a hostel, I would make multiple ascents of Ben Nevis on the Saturday, devour bowls of pasta before sleeping, and repeat on Sunday before driving back to university. When driving to and from Scotland I would go via the Lake District, bring my walking boots and pop up a few fells or roam around the hills near the M74. Once again, the expedition was starting to become a key focus, and regardless of the precarious fundraising situation, I wanted to ensure I was in the right condition if the opportunity did arise.

As April 2010 began to draw ever closer, our fundraising

attempts were not looking any better. Despite securing good potential media coverage, the fear that the expedition would have to be delayed by a year became very real. The weather window to climb Everest is tight. If it was not to be April 2010 then the only alternative would be April 2011. I tried not to think that way.

The Chinese philosopher Lao Tzu said, 'Be careful what you water your dreams with. Water them with worry and fear and you will produce weeds that choke the life from your dream. Water them with optimism and solutions and you will cultivate success. Always be on the lookout for ways to turn a problem into an opportunity for success. Always be on the lookout for ways to nurture your dream.'

Luck is the element that often gets overlooked when it comes to fundraising and sponsorship. Still, as the former professional golfer and nine-time major winner, Gary Player, said, 'The more I practice, the luckier I get.' On the whole, hard work puts the odds of luck happening in one's favour as much as possible. By developing my brand and social outreach, my chances of fundraising success were heavily increased. I wrote letters to pretty much anyone that might be interested. Often it is not that person who will sponsor you but someone they know, or even a link beyond that.

Stuart Mitchell was the guy who came to my rescue and enabled my Everest 2010 expedition to take place. A former St Andrews student and a keen climber, Stuart runs S. W. Mitchell Capital LLP, a European equities investment boutique based in London. We spoke at length about what I was trying to achieve, the plans I had in place in terms of targeted publicity, and how he would gain from the relationship. His intelligence and business prowess was unquestionable. Being the first investor on a project is the hardest part. It is easy to jump on board something with momentum which is heading in the right direction, but for him to take a punt on a 20-year-old kid with a dream was bold and I am enormously grateful for his faith.

Having the financial element secured was an unrivalled relief. It enabled Freddie to direct his efforts to maximising the brand and me to focus properly on the climb preparations. I wrote more letters to people I respected, both to get their support and tap them for knowledge. I read one of Jeremy Clarkson's articles in *The Times* about the hellishness of life in a tent. He wrote cynically, as only Clarkson can, about the sheer frustration and discomfort of a camping holiday with his family – a frozen zip, the morning dew collapsing down from the roof of the tent onto a dozing camper and the hassle of erecting the thing. I wrote to him for my own amusement and because he was a patron of Help for Heroes. He gave a helpful response about media advice but more entertainingly added, 'I think you are completely mad and have absolutely no jealousy of what you are about to undertake. Equally, I wish you the best of luck and safety in your endeavours while thanking you for supporting Help for Heroes.'

Jeremy Clarkson's physical exploits were not necessarily the first thing that came to mind when I thought of him. As a passionate smoker and motorhead, I would not say he represented the epitome of human physical endeavour but was rather someone I appreciated in his own field. Two people that I did have huge respect for were Sir Ranulph Fiennes and Bear Grylls. Bear, because it was his book *Facing Up* that inspired me to embark on this journey, as well as for his TV programmes and work as Chief Scout for The Scout Association. It is hard not to look up to Sir Ranulph Fiennes. Deemed the 'world's greatest living explorer' by the *Guinness Book of World Records*, his achievements are as impressive as they are numerous. Following on from a successful career in the British Army and the SAS, he has undertaken some of the most daring and adventurous expeditions ever. He was the first man to visit both the North and South Poles by surface means and the first to completely cross Antarctica unsupported and on foot. As well as that, he discovered the lost city of Ubar in Oman, climbed Mount Everest, ran the Marathon des Sables and completed seven marathons in seven days in seven continents. He is one of a kind. I wrote to them both asking for their advice and also for them to be patrons of my Seven Summits attempt. To my surprise and delight, both responded positively.

I wish Geordie all the success and safety in this epic challenge. It is an endeavour that will take him to the limits and probably beyond, and that sort of commitment is hard not to admire! Thank you for supporting him and Help for Heroes.

Bear Grylls

An ambitious young man with genuine determination, Geordie's attitude is inspiring and I am proud to support his challenge. I wish him all the best in this record attempt and for his exciting future as an explorer.

Sir Ranulph Fiennes

Their support meant an enormous amount personally but it also added legitimacy to what I was trying to achieve. By lending their names to the project they gave the expedition a wider appeal.

For so long Everest had remained a goal that was unattainable, beyond reach and out of my grasp. Unlike the other mountains, people had heard of Everest, heard of George Mallory and of Edmund Hillary. They knew the stories of bodies on the mountainside and of moments of hardship and endeavour on the slopes of the highest mountain on earth. People often viewed Everest as a pinnacle of achievement – 'What is your Everest?' as the phrase goes. But this was my Everest, my journey and my sole ambition.

I continued to read and learn about the mountain and the challenges that lay ahead. I spoke to as many people as possible about their experiences and what they would have done differently. Everyone had a different take on what was required to stand on the summit. For some it was simple advice like, 'Just grit your teeth, put your head down and keep putting one foot in front of the other.' Others said, 'Pray for good weather, good luck and take the opportunity when it comes.' It was good advice but I wanted to understand the mountain, its characteristics and what made summiting that peak so difficult. I knew coping with altitude would be the main area of concern and that is what I questioned people on most. As well as meeting hardy and seasoned mountaineers, I also met with people who had failed on previous Everest attempts and those who were embarking on a similar endeavour to me.

Bonita was one of those and, after being put in touch, we met for a coffee. She was a few years older than me and was aiming to become the youngest British female to climb Everest. She had also worked hard to attain sponsorship for her climb. There is often an air of cynicism about how young people manage to get the money to go on these big expeditions. The wider perception is that we all have a silent backer or parents who fund it. Although that is sometimes the case, with Bonita I knew it wasn't and exchanging stories with her about our parallel stories was reassuring. She had been climbing for less time than me but immediately felt a huge passion for it and had diligently prepared.

She was climbing with the British guide, Kenton Cool, who, despite charging a large amount for his climbs on the Nepalese side of the mountain, had enviable success rates for both summits and safety. Bonita and I purchased small Union flags from a tourist shop in Windsor to take to the summit. The shopkeeper was cynical when we explained what we needed them for after we were 20p short of the right change. After showing him our websites, he gave them to us and wished us luck and safety. Bonita and I offered one another solidarity and encouragement as we each tried to achieve this ambitious goal in our own way.

I was climbing with an Adventure Peaks team again and googled who I would be spending the next few months with. We had an ex-England rugby player, an Army Officer and a Royal Marine as well as a firefighter, a diver and a dentist. As with all expeditions to date, the team covered a wide spectrum of ages, experiences and motivations.

Matt and Pete were both young, 26 and 28 respectively, and were also climbing for Help for Heroes as well as for the John Thornton Young Achievers Foundation (JTYAF), a charity established in memory of their mutual friend, John

Thornton, who had died while serving in Afghanistan in 2008. Matt was in the Royal Marines and the tagline of the charity was, 'Climb as high as you can dream – helping young people to achieve their ambitions.'

Having emailed a few times before the expedition, I watched their YouTube training video and, sensing that as well as being motivated they had a good sense of humour, I felt an immediate affinity. I would not get the opportunity to meet any of my teammates before seeing them at Heathrow or Kathmandu, but was reassured by the skillset and mentality of the people in the team. The pressures of high altitude would reveal people's true characteristics. Big mountains can do that. Time spent together when the stakes are rising and the pressures mounting reveals what people are really like.

———————

The past six months had certainly involved ups and downs with family, fundraising, training and academics, but I was fortunate to have a strong group around me who believed in what I was doing. As much as stresses on big mountains reveal people's character, I also found that my focus on my climbs had unforeseen consequences in terms of relationships with people. I had become increasingly dedicated to the Seven Summits; I had to be or it simply would not have happened. I often isolated myself from what the majority of my friends were doing. Again, I felt I had to give myself the time and space to get all the right ducks aligned.

Klara and I stayed together, albeit in an occasionally haphazard and tumultuous way. She was the person with whom I could genuinely express my fears and ambitions. I knew her love for me was authentic and it gave me strength knowing she believed so strongly in me. As time went on, she and Freddie would develop a platonic, unspoken bond through mutual concern and desire for my success, both before and during expeditions. These endeavours were team efforts. Although I was climbing, it was everything that happened around it which enabled my efforts.

I had farewell drinks in St Andrews and was touched by how many people turned up. Perhaps it was students looking for any excuse to have a party, but it was also because of their kindness and consideration. Saying goodbye to many of them until the summer was odd. I knew most people would continue with their daily lives and occasionally look at my blog, but there was an unspoken anxiety about Everest and people wrote me incredibly reflective and thoughtful messages and letters. I greatly appreciated every word I received. I read and reread them night after night. But I was intrigued to note there was a sense of cautious apprehension in how people dealt with me going away. It was as though they wanted to make sure they had made their peace and written their words of wisdom in case anything happened to me – a cleansing of their conscience. Was it about their own peace of mind, or was it to give me extra strength for when I needed to delve into my reserves? I took them at face value, treasured their kindness and used their support as extra motivation.

I was often asked about fear of death and the risk of going on big expeditions. I would nonchalantly respond with lines such as, 'The risk of death is everywhere... You can get hit by a car and die tomorrow.' That was missing the point and I knew it. High-altitude mountaineering, even if one takes the standard routes, is a dangerous game. Chris, my guide on

Elbrus, had died in an avalanche in Scotland. Heidi, my guide on Denali, had died in an avalanche in Colorado. Both were seasoned climbers, in areas they were familiar with, and yet fate transpired against them. I was aware of the risks, perhaps that was part of the appeal, but I certainly did not want to die. I assured myself that one really should not die on big mountains, that it represented either foolishness or extreme misfortune. It was easy to say so from the comfort of my living room in the UK, but both foolishness and misfortune are regular occurrences at altitude that have cut short the lives of many great climbers.

The departure date was looming and I drove home in a contemplative mood. I enjoy driving, especially through beautiful scenery, and I find that switching the radio off and cruising along a motorway in quietness can be hugely reflective. Returning home to a chaotic mess of letters, sponsorship flags and new kit was exciting as much as it was daunting. My kit was spread about all over the place, much to the despair of my mum, who dealt with the departure stress in her own inimitable manner. Mum knows very little of big mountains or the adventure world, not just because of a fear of heights, but because it is not one of her passions. With the other mountains, she had not heard of them and they did not represent danger in her mind. She did, however, know about Everest. Her concern for the impending trip was evident.

I had waited a long time for this opportunity. I'd had a picture of the North Face of Everest on the wall above my bed for a number of years, since the idea of climbing the mountain came to my head. It seemed an impossibility just getting there. I was excited to see the mountain for the first time, I was excited to tie up my crampons and grip the ice for the first time. I was excited to see how my body and mind would cope when put to the test.

I found the human psychology aspect of sporting and endurance endeavours fascinating. I had felt inspired to write to Ranulph Fiennes after watching a candid one-hour interview with him on the BBC. At the time, I struggled to comprehend his true motivations for going on these pioneering exploratory expeditions. He would bat the question off by saying it was to beat the Norwegians to the prize, something that obviously appealed to national pride. I could not accept this as the real answer. Through my own endeavours I wanted to understand my reasons and perhaps, when put in extreme situations, I would uncover that further.

I wanted to know whether I would have the strength to persevere when the going got tough. I wanted to know whether I had the moral courage to make the difficult decision to turn back or head for the top. My previous expeditions had taught me a great deal but I had still felt within myself mentally and physically. There were certainly times when I had needed *sisu*, had pushed pretty deep and fought away the negative thoughts that crossed my mind. There were times when I was cold and sleep-deprived but I still felt I had not been truly tested. I was fascinated to find out what my psychological and physiological limits were and how I would react.

Much to Mum's relief, I packed my kit a few days in advance. This avoided the usual bombsite that greeted us both before departure day and I felt ready to go. I said a tearful goodbye at home before heading to Heathrow with Dad and Klara – the difficulties of divorcing parents added an amusingly farcical element to logistics. Saying goodbye to Dad, who had been unwavering in his belief from the inception of the idea, and Klara, who had supported and loved me so fervently over the past six months, was difficult. I knew I would miss her warmth and thoughtfulness. I felt both sadness and guilt as we parted. It is often easier being the one going on a grand journey; there is a huge void in those left behind. Klara and my family would have their own emotional struggles while I was away and the knowledge of that did nothing to relieve my sadness at parting.

Blog – 3 April 2010

I should start with a few thank yous. Thank you to my main sponsor S.W. Mitchell Capital for supporting me. Getting here would have been impossible without you and I am hugely grateful for your support, I will do my absolute best to get your banner to the top.

Thank you to all my friends for supporting me in this venture. Thank you Freddie for all you have done, it would have been an absolute nightmare without your presence.

Lastly, thank you Klara and my family. You have put up with more than anyone else, from tantrums about this and that to the exhilaration that comes with all my previous summits and the anguish in the final few months' preparation for Everest. None of you have ever questioned what I am trying to achieve and I will put all the confidence you have given me into those final few steps to the top of the world.

I have prepared the best way I know how. I am physically in the best shape I have been. I am mentally ready for whatever challenges this mountain throws at me over the course of this expedition.

As for the opportunity part; I know how lucky I am to be given an opportunity to climb to the highest point on earth. There won't be many other 20 year olds on the mountain and I intend to grasp that opportunity with anything and everything I have.

Saying that, I am also 100 percent aware that getting to the top will mean nothing if I can't recount my tale at the other end!

9

EVEREST 2010

8,848m / 29,029ft

Nobody climbs mountains for scientific reasons. Science is used to raise money for the expeditions, but you really climb for the hell of it.

Edmund Hillary

The routine of nervous and awkward encounters with team-mates at the airport had become the norm but Everest was different again. Almost everyone had a blog of some kind to keep their friends and family in the loop so we had all done background research on each other. There was the usual line of enquiry about previous expedition experience but nobody wanted to give too much away. Nobody wanted to come across as too brash or cocky – it isn't the British way.

But we had all made the choice to go with Adventure Peaks, and to climb from China, which gave us some understanding of each other's perspective. Statistically, climbing from China made no sense. The weather was consistently colder and windier, the potential summit days were fewer, the success rate was lower and the death rate was higher. No logical person would climb that route. However, logic usually comes in second place to necessity and I couldn't afford to pay double the cost to climb from Nepal. With that price came huge benefits to greatly increase one's chances of success, but in the financial position I was in, I had no choice. By virtue of the fact that my teammates were in the same boat, I felt confident that we would not have any of the Everest prima donnas that I had read so much about.

By the time the flight departed, we had scoped each other out and had some idea of how we were planning to tackle the impending challenge. Discussions about how much oxygen we would use quickly came up. To climb a mountain without supplementary oxygen is the purest way of reaching the summit. Genetically very few people have the capability to accomplish such a feat and to reach a height of 8,848m without is an astonishing feat. Before Reinhold Messner and Peter Habeler summited Everest in 1978 without oxygen, people thought it was an impossibility, that humans were simply unable to function in that environment. Messner wanted to prove his doubters wrong a second time and in 1980 he pioneered a new route up the North Face, via the Norton Couloir, solo and without oxygen.

By signing up to a professionally led but non-guided expedition, we acknowledged we were not going to be Reinhold Messner. We acknowledged we were not going to be George

Mallory, who ventured higher than was considered possible at the time. We also acknowledged we were not going to be discovering new routes or breaking speed records. But our own personal journeys were going to be bold or challenging in their own way. Everyone who climbs a mountain has to be true to themselves about the approach they take. I had known people lie about how they had climbed a mountain due to embarrassment, or perhaps guilt that they were not as pioneering as they led people to believe. Whatever level of support you require, I believe you need to be comfortable sharing that. With my levels of experience, this non-guided expedition was the right balance of challenge and support.

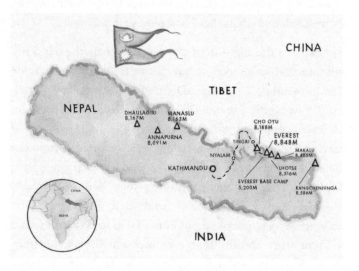

Arriving in the capital city of Nepal was as manic as expected. Spring is the busiest time of year for tourism, one of the country's key sources of income. One of my best mates from St Andrews was more jealous of my sojourn in Kathmandu than he was of the climbing phase; he loved the craziness, vibrancy and noise of the city. One's senses are constantly on high alert from the screeching of motorbike horns combined with the dust and the crowds. Amid that chaos are beautiful side streets, alleyways that open out into calming waterways and an atmosphere of adventure among all the tourists. People rarely go to Kathmandu to stay there but rather as a springboard to explore the country and its magical scenery. That creates a symphony of like-minded people primed to go on the next step of their adventure. I needed to get hold of a few extra bits and bobs for the expedition, which unlocked the door for a whole new challenge, haggling with locals. It can become quite tiresome over an extended period, but if you approach it in the right mood, employing negotiation strategies and trying to beat the best in the business becomes quite a satisfying task.

In Kathmandu, we met the non-British members of our team which included Brendan, a chilled-out Australian who had been living and climbing in Chamonix for the past six months; Max, a free-spirited young American; Scott and Don, a father-son team from Texas; Jasper, a slick Dutch banker; and Heather, a Canadian who worked in London. It was a suitably diverse and certainly energising mix, suggesting that the next few months would be as interesting as they were demanding. At our hotel, we were introduced to the oxygen equipment we would be using higher up, the TopOut mask. With the simplicity of warm weather and no mitts, the system appeared simple enough, but we all knew that higher up would be the real test.

Our departure day from Kathmandu was delayed because of permits which meant a chance to relax before making our move. Finally, we left heading for Friendship Bridge, the Nepal–China border. When climbing from Nepal, you fly to Lukla airport at 2,820m and trek from there to Base Camp at

5,200m. For people trekking to Everest Base Camp, that is the route, meaning it is quite crowded but a well-researched and enjoyable path. If you are climbing from China, however, the only way to Base Camp is a four-day drive, stopping at various local towns en route.

Diary – 7 April 2010

Note to self: Never sit above the wheel arch of a bus in Nepal. Sore ass, dodgy driving, steep cliffs – cracking views! Certainly memorable.

The drive to Friendship Bridge was chaotic. Cars and vans with stickers on the back saying 'IT'S NOT A RACE, DRIVE SAFE' would kiss the apex of a blind corner and hang the back wheels over a precipice. As we gained height, the road meandered magically along the hillside and, despite the car wreckages visible below, it was a glorious journey. Upon entering China, thankfully our visas were accepted, the roads became smooth tarmac (built for the 2008 Beijing Olympics) and it became a positively serene experience. Acclimatisation involved two nights in Nyalam and two more in Tingri at 4,300m on the Tibetan plateau before we would make the final drive to Everest Base Camp at 5,200m.

We caught the first sight of our objective. As barren dusty peaks stretched beyond our sight, suddenly there emerged a dark, imposing pyramid. There it was... Mount Everest! It was easy to believe that we were looking at the highest mountain on earth. Uninviting, daunting and undiminished, yet there was a magnetic draw that made me want to get closer and climb on its slopes.

When George Mallory came to climb Everest in the 1920s,

he wrote about Tingri in less than glowing terms. Tingri is still something of a Wild West town, with a single street on a dusty plain, its one distinguishing feature being a restless and seemingly limitless army of stray dogs. We heard stories of previous climbers being bitten by rabid dogs, ending their Everest attempt before it had started. As such, we would not venture outside without walking poles and an uncompromising attitude as the drooling droves encircled every move we made.

The saving grace for Tingri at least was that we could stretch our legs and have an acclimatisation trek in the surrounding area. It was impossible not to marvel at the space and size of the region as some of the highest mountains in the world came into view including Cho Oyu, sixth highest at 8,188m and Shishapangma, 14th highest at 8,027m.

Ten days after our flight to Nepal we arrived at Base Camp, our home for the next two months. It was a flat, rocky landscape dotted with pockets of brightly coloured tents, all representing climbers hoping to fulfil their ambitions. The North Face loomed over us day and night, serving to remind us of our own insignificance and the magnitude of the task that lay in wait.

We were able to choose any of the 20 unassigned tents. I took one as far away from the central mess tent as possible, one with an unimpeded view of Everest. It appealed to my introverted side and I wanted to wake up and go to sleep with the objective in front of me and to remind myself to savour these precious moments. The view from the back of my tent was the same view as the picture on my wall for all those years. The story had come full circle, in a way, and, instead of relying on other people's pictures and other people's memories, I was about to begin my own Everest story. I blissfully watched as the mountain changed form almost daily. I would wake to find it covered in a fresh white coating and watch as the sun shimmered on its new guise. I gazed up as blue skies emerged overheard, except for a steady stream of clouds moving along the Northeast Ridge and whipping off the summit slopes. I continually wondered what it would be like up there. *What would that wind feel like when it's raging at 8,800m?*

When we had all arrived at Base Camp, we had our oxygen saturation levels and heart rates monitored by a pulse oximeter. At high altitude, there is much less oxygen available to breathe. A pulse oximeter could help determine whether we would have a health issue. The human body performs best at sea level and, as we climbed higher and potentially all the way to the summit, our oxygen saturation levels – the amount of oxygen in our blood – would continue to decrease. As the oxygen level drops, it is harder to breathe and movement is severely reduced. Over the coming months we would slowly acclimatise, giving our bodies time to adjust to breathing less oxygen. The effects of high altitude on humans are considerable. It can lead to medical problems, from the mild symptoms of acute mountain sickness (AMS) to the potentially fatal high altitude pulmonary edema (HAPE) and high altitude cerebral edema (HACE). The higher the altitude, the greater the risk.

The pulse oximeter maxes at 100 percent, and the reading for healthy people at sea level is around 95 percent or higher. A normal first exposure at Base Camp might be in the 80s; it would then drop into the 60s or potentially lower as we climbed higher. We became obsessive, and competitive, to see who had what numbers. In reality, none of us wanted a concerningly low result.

I had already formed a good bond with Matt and Pete. I instinctively trusted them both and looked forward to being alongside them higher up the mountain. Their reasons for being there were inspired by the death of a friend and together they sought to climb in his memory. A strong friendship had taken them to the summit of Aconcagua and, like me, had required them to navigate the whirlwind of sponsorship proposals and fundraising. They were not there for the fame or kudos, but rather to achieve a long-awaited goal and now they had adequate reason to make the commitment.

Upon arriving at Base Camp, Matt was sombre and downbeat. He spoke to the doctor and our team leader, Stu, a double Everest summiteer, about breathing difficulties. For someone so resilient, it was strange seeing him so vulnerable. His saturation levels had dipped to a worrying level, around 60 percent. If you listened closely to his breathing, he said, there was a gentle gargling sound, a sure sign of HAPE, where excess fluid develops in the lungs. This essentially means his body was not able to perform gaseous exchange properly and could not therefore get enough oxygen to function normally. Treatment for HAPE is fairly unwavering: immediate descent and a regular dose of dexamethasone.

As a team we knew, once we had heard the symptoms, that there was only one solution. I spoke with him a few times and he was devastated; he knew what it meant. He did not need to tell me; his vacant stare and reddened eyes said it all. His dream was over and he would be evacuated to Kathmandu the following morning.

It was a gutting start to the expedition for the entire team, losing such a strong and valued member, but especially for Pete. They were old friends and this was very much a project they wanted to complete together. I don't think either of them envisaged standing at the summit without the other. Pete and I spoke a lot and he trusted me enough to be candid and emotional. I empathised with him hugely. His sense of loss would massively impact on his enjoyment and focus during the expedition and I felt an obligation to assist him in the small way I could.

An essential part of any expedition in the Himalayas is the *Puja* – the blessing of the expedition, a ceremony performed by a Lama, a spiritual leader in Tibetan Buddhism, and two or more monks. Those performing a *Puja* ask the Gods for good fortune for the Sherpas and climbers as they attempt to summit the mountain. In front of the altar, offerings are made to the gods and all the critical climbing equipment is blessed – harnesses, crampons and ice axes. Prayer flags are strewn for 30m in several directions. The ceremony closes with the participants sharing food and, finally, with the climbers and Sherpas smearing grey tsampa flour on each other's faces – a symbol of their hope that they may live to see each other when they are old and grey.

We remained at Base Camp for five days before heading up the mountain for the first time. We went for some casual acclimatisation walks up the valley to explore, but for the most part it was a chance to relax and let our bodies do their thing in terms of building up red blood cells. The more time we spent together as a team, the more we understood each other and become cohesive.

Stu, our team leader, had huge amounts of experience. As well as having summited Everest twice, he had summited Broad Peak at 8,051m, Cho Oyu at 8,188m, as well as attempting K2. He had climbed extensively outside the Himalayas, including in the Andes, Alps and Russia. An incredibly unassuming character, he led the team by example through his calmness and humility. He had begun climbing in the Lake District as a child and, for him, mountains big or small were places that gave him the greatest satisfaction in life. His job as team leader meant he would have the final say on who would go for the summit and when. At times it was probably an unenviable task managing the egos and desires of everyone on the team, but Stu projected a sense of composure throughout.

For the first time, we had begun to witness the variable weather on the mountain even here. Fresh snow and strong winds overnight gave a stark reminder of where we were and what we were up against. After stretching the legs a bit we had our first foray to more significant altitudes as we trekked up a frozen river to 6,000m. Josh described it as our first 'dig deep' day. It was not a particularly demanding amble but it was more of a test than we had had before, as well as providing a small insight into different people's approaches.

Brendan, the Aussie, would brazenly head to the front, set a strong pace and go off into the distance. For someone so laidback and measured the majority of the time, when he moved, he went with purpose and appeared to have a natural adaptation to altitude. Some people like to be at the front to appear stronger to others, others to prove to themselves they have the strength – he was probably a mixture of both. On these mountains, you move at a sustainable pace you are comfortable with and see where that leaves you in the pack. Other climbs I had been on, especially those like Denali where we were physically roped together, were very much team efforts and the group made their way up the mountain as a collective.

Everest is very different and this was not a guided expedition. As such, people had the freedom to go at the pace they wanted and meet at the next checkpoint. Some preferred to move as a group while others were more content in their own company. I was pleased to make it to 6,000m, as not everybody did. It gave me a bit of confidence in how I was personally faring. The next phase would be tough and every small psychological boost could provide a percent or two increase in mental fortitude higher up the mountain.

10

A GAME OF RISK

The mountains have rules. They are harsh rules, but they are there.

Walter Bonatti

We trekked the 16 miles of rocky debris covering the East Rongbuk Glacier and it felt as though we were finally making progress up the mountain. From Advanced Base Camp we could see the route up ahead. The Headwall leading to the North Col at 7,000m would be the next obstacle during Phase One of our three-phased approach to make the summit. The Headwall is an ominously steep and imposing section of the route. George Mallory described uncovering the path up the Headwall as, 'The key that unlocked the door to Everest.' We reached Crampon Corner, threw on our crampons and harnesses, moved across an icy plateau and stared upwards. This would split the team and provide the sternest test yet by far.

It was a pleasure to get the crampons and high-altitude boots on and hear them bite into the crisp shimmering ice. The sun was beating down remorselessly but this was why we were here; to see how we would stack up against nature. The highest I had been before was the summit of Aconcagua at 6,962m so reaching the North Col would be a new altitude personal best.

It was hard to find a routine that worked. I would move five steps, an odd number to alternate the resting leg, before waiting for about 10 breaths. My mind was willing my body to move more efficiently but the steep gradient and thin altitude wouldn't allow it. I pleaded with my body to increase the tempo or number of steps but the environment denied it. There was a fixed rope but that did not detract from the physical demands on our bodies. High altitude mountaineering is not a spectator sport – it is often a battle between the ears of each climber as they strain to maintain momentum.

We would stop every so often to rest, hydrate and eat before hauling our bodies up in preparation to move again. Pete and I traded step for step before coming across the first of two major crevasses. These deep cracks in the ice of a glacier have always given me a sense of foreboding as they loom menacingly below, bringing about feelings of fear and emptiness. I remember Bear's story on Everest about him falling into one and being rescued by a Sherpa. I had read *Touching the Void* about Joe Simpson's courageous struggle to survive after falling into one. Lying across each crevasse were ladders roped together to enable our safe passage. With trepidation, we edged our way across leaving only a small chimney to shuffle up before getting to the North Col.

It was a good moment and I could understand what Mallory meant. The route suddenly opened up and there, 1,800m higher, was the summit of Everest. Rather than remaining at arm's length, it suddenly appeared achievable, despite the exhaustion I was feeling. We made it down to Base Camp after a successful first venture onto Everest proper.

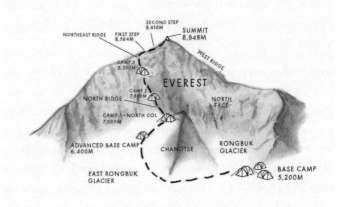

When we were at ABC we received some fairly confronting news. An overhanging serac, a tall peak of ice on the surface of a glacier, had fallen on a team of Hungarian climbers, killing two and severely injuring another. The news was unconfirmed so we had to remain quiet until the climbers were identified and their loved ones could be told. Websites such as *EverestNews* and *Explorersweb* tracked expeditions and would compile reports from teams and individuals about progress on Himalayan expeditions. If families and friends heard drips of information about climbers dying on the Headwall, knowing we were heading up there, alarm bells would start ringing.

The three Hungarian climbers were very experienced but it was sheer misfortune. 'Mountains are not fair or unfair, they are just dangerous,' according to Reinhold Messner. Even if you put all the safety parameters in place, sometimes circumstances are beyond your control. Nobody could have foreseen when that serac was going to fall. For years the fixed lines had wound beneath it without tragedy, but suddenly, when three climbers were there, it collapsed and ended the lives of the two men. I felt for the remaining climber and felt dearly for all their families who would receive this life-changing news.

Spin it however you want, but what we were doing was dangerous. As Brendan said after the incident, 'It is something that every mountaineer considers when they head up a mountain and they deal with that in their own way.' A matter of weeks before I had heard news of an avalanche on the south side of the mountain; we could hear it set off even from our Base Camp. I thought of Bonita who was in Nepal and hoped for her safety. I asked my family to check on her blog to reassure me she was OK, even if there was nothing I could do – fate had already taken its course.

This sort of incident did nothing to appease the fears of our families and friends. I did my best to explain to them the risk management and how safety measures had increased but I did not want them to know how I really felt. Luck was a key factor and it worried me that things outside my control could alter or indeed terminate my life. I knew my family, Klara, and friends would worry. I knew they would be getting on with their lives but every so often my safety and their fears would be stark. They just had to trust my judgement and find faith that I would make it through.

I visited the Everest memorial at Base Camp during one of our rest days. Some people did so immediately after arriving but I wanted to be on the mountain and to understand it better first. There were names that I had read about; stories of courage, pioneering spirit and human weakness.

Some resonated with me more than others; David Sharp was one of those. I had read about his death in Nick Heil's book *Dark Summit*, which covered the 2006 Everest season. Eleven climbers died on Everest that year, most of them on the north. They died not in a single storm as they had in 1996 (a year when 15 climbers lost their lives, eight of them on a single day), but in a series of unfolding tragedies. Sharp died alone, in a cave on the Northeast Ridge, from extreme altitude sickness and exposure. His death was highly controversial as more than 40 climbers had passed him while he was still alive, en route to the summit.

It was Sharp's third attempt on Everest after trying unsuccessfully in 2003 and 2004. He had opted to go with a questionable local company, Asian Trekking, that provided minimal expedition support but with minimal cost. He had wanted to attempt the mountain without the use of supplementary oxygen, without Sherpa support and, on summit day, without even a radio to call for help. After neglecting to turn around late in the day, Sharp continued and may or may not have reached the summit. On his descent in the dark, at about 8,500m, he was forced to bivouac under a rocky overhang known as Green Boots Cave. Without supplementary oxygen, on a very cold night, David Sharp, likely suffering from extreme frostbite, altitude sickness and exhaustion, was unable to continue his descent and subsequently died.

The story shocked me. I had been exhausted at altitude before but I had no idea what it was like to be up there at that altitude and did not know how I would cope. I was tearful as I looked at the plaque that read:

DAVID SHARP
1972-2006
SLEEP SERENE AMID THE SNOWS UNTROD

This brought my fears and concerns to the fore. How does one cope when the cold seeps so deep into your core that you can barely move? What was he thinking as he sat there in that cave? Why could he not force himself up to survive? Would I have the strength to continue if I was stranded up there or I would be forced to give up like David Sharp did? Would I sacrifice my only chance of summiting Everest to assist someone who was almost dead? Would my teammates assist me if I was physically and mentally spent at 8,600m?

I reflected also on the memorial of Tony Swierzy, the former SAS soldier, who died in 1984 and those of Pete Boardman and Joe Tasker, who died on their bold expedition in May 1982. These were experienced and strong climbers whose lives had ended prematurely. There was a memorial for Tsewang Paljor, the Indian policeman who died in 1996 and whose body, now known as 'Green Boots', lay in the cave that David Sharp had died in at 8,500m, and had done for almost 15 years. And then, set apart from the rest, were the memorials for Mallory and Irvine.

IN MEMORY OF GEORGE LEIGH MALLORY AND
ANDREW IRVINE LAST SEEN 8 JUNE 1924
AND ALL THOSE WHO DIED DURING THEIR
PIONEERING BRITISH MOUNT EVEREST EXPEDITION

Mallory and Irvine were true legends of Everest and heroes
of mine. Their memory was wrapped in mystery, and a spirit
of comradeship and boldness. Part of the appeal of climbing
from the north was following the same route that they
pioneered almost a century before. It was Mallory's third
attempt on Everest and Irvine's first; he was only 22 years
old. Fellow expedition member, Noel Odell, spotted the two
climbing a prominent rock step, either the First or Second
Step, before his whole fascinating vision vanished as the
pioneering climbers were enveloped in a cloud once more.
Their fate, and whether or not they made the summit, has
been debated in tents and pubs around the world ever since.

―――――――

At Base Camp, the news of the Hungarians had brought
about introspection amongst all the teams. The bodies had
been recovered, their remaining belongings located and the
surviving climber evacuated back to Kathmandu. A sombre
and reflective mood was prevalent. We knew that just a day
before, it had been our team crossing beneath that serac. We
knew it could just as easily have been one or more of us.

It made me miss home. It was natural to question what I was
doing but the banality of life back in Hampshire, London or
St Andrews was something I craved in an odd way. I had
only been away a month but the knowledge that I was only
halfway through this trip brought its own demands. I

wanted to know how Hattie, our joyous golden retriever, was doing. I wanted gossip from the topsy-turvy world of student relationships and I wanted to know whether Newcastle United had won the league.

I had photos of my family and friends stuck around the inside of my tent in the knowledge that their presence would give me the boost I needed. I longed to hold onto Klara, tell her how much I loved her, and see her pride when I returned home successfully. I looked forward to devouring Mum's fish pie, still the best I've had, when I got home and could talk nonsense with my sisters over the breakfast table. I was excited about going for a walk with Hattie. I couldn't wait to get home, mow the lawn and sit outside with a gin and tonic, roll a cigarette and know I had reached the summit of Everest. All of that was seemingly a world away. I was still in a sleeping bag, on a Thermarest, alone in a tent at over 5,000m. I was still peeing into a one-litre Nalgene water bottle before I went to bed and using it as a hot-water bottle. I was still living off a diet involving excess spam and lychees while chugging around eight litres of water per day to remain hydrated. Crucially as well, I was still many weeks and much hardship away from standing at the summit of *Chomolungma*.

One huge positive was the return of Matt from Kathmandu. His HAPE had been severe but, through persistence and charm, he had somehow blagged his way out of hospital, found a driver and made his way back to Base Camp. Quite how he managed it logistically, not to mention physically, was beyond me. He had visibly lost a lot of weight and looked a modified version of his former muscular self. For all of us it was great to see him back, but none more so than Pete. I had spent much of the past few weeks with my ginger-haired, tweed-cap-wearing friend, and had developed a huge sense of trust and loyalty with him. We climbed together and provided each other with the support that one needs on this sort of expedition. I think we were all cautious about getting too optimistic. Matt was certainly not one to raise expectations unduly. However, by making the decision to return to Base Camp, he had also made the decision to return to the mountain proper.

Everest draws a broad range of intrepid and restless souls to challenge themselves on its slopes. Jon Krakauer said, 'The self-selection process tends to weed out the cautious and the sensible in favour of those who are single-minded and incredibly driven.' Everyone wants to summit Everest for their own personal reasons; each one of us had made a commitment. We had each seen a picture of Everest or read a book and thought: 'Yep, I want to do that, I want to be that person,' and booked it. Not everyone is willing to take that step. At Base Camp, Brendan interviewed a few members of the team about their motivations for putting their life at risk to summit Everest. Combined with discussions around the mess tent, these were illuminating as to the psychology behind people's attempts.

On Everest, more than any other mountain, the challenge element seemed to be key. Yes, there might be a desire to bolster the CV for some, to spin a yarn back to mates at the local pub or make a nice photo album. On the whole, though, the desire seemed to be simply to see if it was possible. People wanted to test themselves, to see if they could commit and follow through with a seemingly impossible dream.

For others, it was a true love of climbing, something that had been part of their life for as long as they could remember. The simple joy of being in the hills brought about their interest in mountaineering and then, in time, the allure of Everest got bigger and bigger. It was that itch that needed scratching.

Some pure climbers say that they don't want to climb Everest because of its commercialisation. The crowds mean summiting is meaningless now and you can pay your way to the top. I think that's a lie. A friend said to me once, 'Every kid has at some stage thought about climbing Mount Everest. They might ditch the idea totally or keep putting it off, but the thought is there. That's why it's appealing.'

11

CABIN FEVER

If you can wait and not be tired of waiting...

Rudyard Kipling

The next step would be to spend a few nights at the North Col, climb as high as we could up the North Ridge and then return. Mentally we thought it would be quite demanding as the novelty of Phase One was gone but equally, it was not the final push. Back up the East Rongbuk Glacier – 16 miles is a pretty hefty stint in one go at that altitude. I broke it up with regular stops, audiobooks including Paddy Leigh Fermor's *A Time of Gifts* and a pleasant mixture of Shania Twain and the Rolling Stones.

The relief of arriving at ABC was spread across each person's face as they entered the mess tent. Our group of individuals thrown together had become more of a team.

We started to take genuine pleasure from teammates making it and appearing strong. We had genuine concern if others appeared to be struggling. However, despite the teamwork, it still remained a battle within each of our own minds to make the summit. Nobody else was going to take those steps. Nobody else was going to cast aside what Ranulph Fiennes would call 'the wimpish voice of negativity' that tells you to stop when you have to carry on.

Our team would soon begin to splinter off as the expedition demands took their toll. It is a harsh environment and the reality of the demands required dawned on different people at different times. Jasper appeared to be everything you would want in an adventurer and had the talk to match it. Speaking with knowledge and poise, there was an air about him that crept into arrogance but it appeared justified. He had the watch manufacturer sponsorship, he had the high-tech clothing sponsorship, he had the relationship with *National Geographic* and Canon photography.

When he decided to call it a day at ABC it was still a surprise. He had been ill with a stomach bug for a few days and I think the reality of the challenge was not aligned with his desire to reach the summit. To achieve the summit of a big mountain it requires each climber to endure, to suffer and to really crave the end result. I respected Jasper but I don't think he wanted it enough and he left the team discreetly. He said months later on his blog that, 'This accident [the Hungarians] would turn out to be a prelude for the season. High altitude sickness, quick shifts of weather and long-lasting summit winds were the reasons I could not reach the summit.' Jasper created his own script as to why he called it a day. In the words of Hermann Buhl, 'Mountains have a way of dealing with overconfidence.'

Scott and Don also decided to end it at ABC, which was less of a surprise. They were a Texan father-and-son team who were always kind and positive. They dreamed of climbing the Seven Summits and together had reached the highest point on four of the seven continents. In many ways it was the dream father-and-son pursuit, but, given Don's age and their consistent lack of speed, together they decided enough was enough. It was a shame to see them make that decision but it was also the right one. Still, they had made the decision to give it a go when others would choose the easier option of not putting their head above the parapet. It may not have resulted in the outcome they envisaged but they would never have known that unless they had given it a shot.

———

Back up the Headwall we went, with alarmingly heavy packs. We were to spend two nights there as well as caching food and kit needed for the final summit push. It was going to be another day, in the words of Andy, a proud Hull resident and teammate, 'of hard graft'. Back to Crampon Corner, back to the base of the Headwall and, once again, a day of enduring the relentless heat that sapped our precious energy reserves. We wished it would relent; but be careful what you wish for. After spending the evening boiling snow to hydrate and getting calories on board for the slog up the North Ridge in the morning, we woke to heavy snowfall and strong winds knowing a strenuous few hours lay ahead.

The North Ridge is neither exciting nor mentally stimulating. Our aim was to hit the rocky line at around 7,500m in order to maximise the chances of adapting our bodies to the thinning oxygen levels. Every step would be a new altitude personal best.

The weather was ferocious. A vicious wind cut across the unprotected ridge, whipping up snow in all directions. The heavy clouds meant visibility was negligible and progress was slow. Matt and Pete remained at the North Col, so I headed up with nothing but my own thoughts and doubts for company. A climbing routine was impossible to find and without a clear sense of pace against other people, or any identifiable features, my mind was constantly questioning the purpose. *We don't even have an end goal today. Nobody is going to get to 7,500m anyway so just turn around and be done with it.* That would be countered with, *This is why you're here, idiot. What were you expecting – this is Everest, for Christ's sake. Put your head down and get up the fucking slope.*

I have always struggled with maintaining mental focus and positivity during these climbs. The self-doubt and self-loathing are incredibly raw in my head. I am constantly stuck in my own head questioning why I'm there and why I'm putting myself through this agony. Other climbers I know have such a relentless pursuit of their goal that they don't allow those feelings of negativity to creep in. When my suffering increases I am wholly present in the moment and plagued by querying my choices.

With those conditions and that mental fragility, I did not make it to 7,500m but rather turned around at 7,250m. It was a reasonable effort. Brendan and a few others made it a little higher but the majority barely made it out of Camp 1, such was the unpleasant nature of the weather. Getting back into the tents was a huge relief. Finally, protection between myself and Mother Nature.

A fairly fitful sleep ensued and as early as possible we headed back down the Headwall to the safety of ABC. I emailed Klara and my family from there:

Email to family – 4 May 2010

I am feeling pretty weak at the moment. Heading down to Base Camp today which should be good. I am losing a fair amount of weight up here – apologies Klara but no super beach bod post-Everest I'm afraid. Gonna be a wreck by the end of this sadly. Serious TLC (Tender Loving Care before the Swedish contingent [Klara] asks questions) needed on return I predict.

I need to get to Base Camp and relax. Then one big push and job done. Basically, it is pretty fucking hard out here, harder than I thought it would be.

Anyway, speak tomorrow. I miss you all lots. Love

G x

With relief, I headed down to the oxygen-rich air of Base Camp. It is remarkable how one's body adapts to the altitude over time. Upon first arriving at 5,200m, we all felt fairly poor. But returning now, after a couple of nights at 7,000m, it seemed a congenial place to be with benign conditions and moderate temperatures. Although we had not reached the desired altitude, the main aim of spending a couple of nights at the North Col was done. Phase Two was therefore complete and a relative success.

The rest of the team were faring OK but with varying degrees of comfort. Brendan, Stu and Max seemed consistently resilient and strong but, beyond that, we had all experienced our own worlds of hurt. Pete spent three nights at the North Col to assist Matt in his re-acclimatisation programme; bearing in mind he had been evacuated back to Kathmandu and 7,000m was the highest he had ever been, it was a massive effort. It had taken its toll on them both and I think they hoped we would be delayed a bit before heading back up. Pete's commitment in helping Matt get back on track was admirable – an amazing insight into true friendship and trust.

Without expressing it overtly, I think a lot of the team feared what lay ahead, if the struggle was that great at the North Col.

———

Although we were all making our own progress at our own speeds, we did so within the timeframe that Stu gave us and with the awareness that we had to rely on each other. Brian had earned the nickname the 'Lone Wolf' as a result of his unnecessary and sometimes ludicrous solo endeavours. Showing a concerning lack of teamwork, he would venture off from Base Camp or the North Col without informing anyone and without any means of communication. He seemed set on forging his own schedule at the expense of Stu and the Sherpas. When he did once take a radio he was moving slowly and approaching a cut-off time for making it up the Headwall. As Stu dutifully made this clear to him, Brian opted to turn his radio off and continue upwards. Unsurprisingly, he exhausted himself and it required several Sherpas to re-ascend the Headwall and guide him safely down again. That sort of selfish attitude has no place on a mountain, and certainly not when you are part of a team. If your actions are blatantly compromising the effectiveness and, crucially, the safety of others, then you are a liability. We called him the Lone Wolf in jest but his attitude had the potential to compromise the success of other members of the team.

It was at this stage of the expedition that the Sherpas began to show their unrivalled prowess. Sherpas are an ethnic group living in the Himalayas in Nepal and a select few are chosen as mountain guides. These are the guys who enable climbers to ascend Himalayan peaks and, without them, our attempts would fall at the first hurdle. They are physiologically adapted to the altitude, meaning they do not require the same acclimatisation process as Western climbers, having been born and raised at over 3,000m. The mountains are their domain and learning from them was invaluable. At over 5,000m, they would often have a cigarette in hand – 'Sherpa Oxygen' they called it – as they sauntered by, while we gasped in the thin air. On Edmund Hillary's expedition to climb Everest, beyond the British and New Zealand climbers there were hundreds of Sherpas and yaks assisting them along the way. A key reason Tenzing Norgay was named to climb alongside Hillary was his natural aptitude and experience at altitude.

Our head climbing Sherpa, or *Sirdar*, was Nuru Wangchhu Sherpa. His strength at altitude was baffling and humbling; he had over eight Everest summits as well as numerous other 8,000m peaks to show for it. His team of 10 Sherpas would assist us. Being a Sherpa in Nepal is one of the most profitable and prestigious jobs in a cripplingly poor country. What they earn on one Everest expedition, especially if successful, will put them in the highest income bracket in the country. It is a dangerous profession and one that requires hard work and endurance. For them, however, it is often seen as the only path they will ever have to financial stability and educating their children.

I grew close to a couple of the Sherpas, namely Dorje Khatri and his nephew Sonam Dorje. They never failed to welcome me with a *Namaste*, a huge smile and a high five. I liked them, trusted them enormously and also knew that I would not get remotely close to the summit without their support.

———

Phases One and Two were complete. The team was at Base Camp resting, relaxing and recuperating. I was turning 21 on 5 May and looked forward to speaking to my family for the first time since leaving. I emailed them, Freddie and Klara fairly regularly but had not loosened the purse strings enough to warrant a sat phone call until now. I calculated the time difference of 5 hours 45 minutes from my two dollar watch purchased in Nyalam a month before.

I had a few envelopes in my backpack clearly marked, 'Don't Open Until 5th May'. Thankfully I had resisted and it was worth the wait to open birthday cards from loved ones. Josh took over cooking duties from the chefs for the night and produced the goods for a special memory. For years I had envisaged spending my 21st birthday on Everest, so it was surreal that it had come to fruition. I thought about how most of my mates had spent their birthdays: a big party with a marquee perhaps or a night out in London, and yet, here I was, shivering and sleep-deprived thousands of miles from home – and I would not have wanted it any other way.

The previous week had been a huge drain on my resources. Physically I was tired and had lost a lot of weight due to the sheer amount of calories burnt and the struggle to eat anything at high altitude. A few years before I might have embraced that perhaps but now I rather resented the change. I needed the excess body fat to stay warm. I needed to rebuild muscle to sustain my body higher up. Yet still, even at this location, my mind was unsettled by the struggle of putting on weight. I had made huge progress with my eating disorder and knew I had to get more food on board for the ensuing challenges, but my mind slightly resented what I was doing to my body in terms of mass calorie consumption in a short space of time. My throat was also becoming increasingly painful; I had developed a hacking cough which made breathing complicated. Like many others, I needed a good break before heading up the mountain again.

I had also taken with me a pack of letters which people had written before I set off. Their sentiments, very honest and considerate, were written for different reasons but it was times like this that they made a big difference to my confidence.

Keep going up, my friend. I know you will rise to every challenge out there (and I do not doubt there will be many!) and overcome them with valour, determination and the drive you have already shown. Know that we will all be back in St Andrews making sure everyone is behind you.

May you enjoy your time of musical appreciation with the one and only – Bob Dylan. In his words, 'Take care of your memories, for you cannot relive them' – I hope you can use this throughout your trip. First to keep your own memories safe and then to share with us back home. I will be praying for you every step of the way.

Yours is a friendship I value, we have certainly seen each other on the right and wrong side of fortune. When the peak is done, I will have a pint waiting for you. Enjoy the next couple of months. Stay safe, stay steady, I am sure you will.

Keep following your heart and trust your intuition Geord, they'll leave you in good stead. Have a fantastic time and come back with some great banter.

I would never let you go on this trip unless I knew that you would make it to the top successfully and, most importantly, back safely.

All you need to worry about is moving forward and upward and taking care of yourself. This is a great challenge you are undertaking! If you're ever lonely or cold or feeling helpless, then think of me and all the people that love and support you. We all know you can do this! I can't think of anyone else who could!

Make sure you come back to me my love.

I would read these, and other letters, every day in my tent. They never failed to bring about deep feelings of love and belonging but equally sadness and loneliness. I felt immensely vulnerable, young and exposed on that mountain at times. The length of this expedition was not something I had considered but perhaps my youth had not fully come to terms with the demands I was placing on it.

After a few days of relative comfort and security back at Base Camp, people's morale began to improve. We knew we had done all we could in terms of acclimatising and now we could do nothing but wait for a weather window.

What happens high on the slopes of Mount Everest is largely dependent on jet streams high up in the troposphere. Due to the ongoing rotation of the Earth, jet streams typically travel west to east in both hemispheres between 80–140mph. The summit of Everest at 8,848m is high enough to penetrate the jet stream. For a few weeks in May, the jet stream moves north of the Himalayas, greatly reducing average wind speeds and the chance of precipitation at the top of the mountain. Climbers call the period of calm a weather window.

The lift of the jet stream coincides with the beginning of monsoon season off the coasts of India and Sri Lanka, as winds begin to blow north from the Bay of Bengal. By early June, the monsoon begins to blast the Himalayas with heavy snow and usually brings the end of the climbing season.

Detailed and complicated weather forecasts arrive daily from a variety of sources in the UK, Switzerland and the USA, and teams are often wary about sharing too much information in case it scuppers their own summit plans. It was Stu's job to evaluate these and come up with a strategy for our summit bid. The relevant information was not what was happening now but rather what was going to happen in five days' time – i.e. after our move from Base Camp up to High Camp. Every day was spent hoping for a favourable window, followed by inevitable disappointment when that hope was extinguished.

Meanwhile, using our creativity and resourcefulness we had pub quizzes, film nights, political debates and card games. I had brought the board game Risk with me, which never failed to distract and while away time; if the climb did not show people's true colours, then the merciless necessities for world domination on a board game usually did the trick. Ian surprised (and I think mentally scarred) Heather on her birthday by waking her up in nothing but a Borat mankini, surely a first on Everest. Every breakfast, Jonathan and I pretended to gently press down a cafetière and browse through the Sunday papers but nothing of the kind was within our grasp.

I would read passionately and slowly our team library was stocked up and categorised. I read books on travel, human psychology, crime fiction and everything in between. It was a dream to have the opportunity without distractions – a blessing before the stresses and demands of life got back in the way.

My love for Bob Dylan was satiated by having his book *Chronicles*. In Brendan, I had found another passionate Dylan fan whom I could debate with daily. We would weigh up the antagonistic and politically vibrant days of early-60s Bob versus his electric-guitar-inspired transition half a decade later and compare that to his live performances. We would sit and analyse the anguished lyrics of a true literary genius.

I had also brought Lance Armstrong's book *It's Not About the Bike* (at the time it still featured in the non-fiction section of Waterstones). It was hard not to be inspired by a guy who recovered from testicular cancer and went on to found an amazing charity as well as win seven Tour de France titles back-to-back. I found strength in his words, 'We are so much stronger than we imagine, and belief is one of the most valiant and long-lived human characteristics.' He had seemingly done it all.

I still coveted news from elsewhere and took great pride in hearing my sister had graduated from Edinburgh University, something that seemed totally unattainable for me just then. I wanted to know how Hattie was and what the weather was like in the UK. I felt reassured by Mum's mundane commuting issues and encounters at the supermarket. I wanted to hear about how Bonita was getting on in Nepal.

My condition had improved after three days' rest, as had my throat, and I felt reinvigorated for the third and final phase. The planned weather window on 17–19 May was deemed unsuitable so we would be sitting tight a bit longer. News of successful summits on the south side made us anxious that perhaps we would miss our chance. Stu stayed firm though, and we had to trust him and the forecasts or we would be going in blind.

The Russian team, led by Alex Abramov, decided to celebrate 9 May as Russian Victory Day, a holiday that commemorates the victory of the Soviet Union over Nazi Germany. The cause was obviously something that we Brits could easily get on board with. In an extremely surreal setting, all the climbers on the north side of Everest gathered around for a Russian soiree. Beer, vodka and cognac were flowing aplenty – Dmitry would have been in heaven – and it gave everyone the chance to relax. We all knew that the weather window was unlikely so people let their hair down completely for the first time in months. Some of our team, particularly Stephen, understandably took a fancy to a beautiful medic assisting another team. It turned out she was, in fact, a famous Brazilian model. Needless to say, Stephen's Edinburgh charm had limited success but you couldn't blame the guy for trying.

Email to Family – 12 May 2010

I am getting pretty on edge to be perfectly honest. Unsurprisingly there is a lot of banter that flies around but at this stage in the expedition, it gets to me sometimes. It's all light-hearted of course but I can feel myself getting a bit tetchy. I know I'm not alone either. Cabin fever is setting in. We all just want to get moving.

I miss everyone a lot. I miss a good mate to talk to. I miss my girlfriend. I miss my family.

It is one big push to the top of this bloody mountain and I will put anything and everything into it but before that push, it could well be a pretty challenging week or so.

I just want to get up this thing and back home again.

Love you all. Hugs and kisses.

xx

Waiting at Base Camp too long also increases the fear of losing one's acclimatisation, adding to the tension. Sleeping low for too long means that the red blood cells produced by reaching the higher altitudes begin to normalise again. There was a fear we would have to move back to ABC to re-acclimatise. I struggled with the loneliness and helplessness of the situation. The mountain was beginning to defeat me.

The initial excitement of being back at Base Camp had certainly worn off after two weeks. Everyone was dealing with the pressure in their own way. Some people went for long walks – obviously the Lone Wolf was one of them – while others boxed to expend some energy. There were yogis, sunbathers, readers, writers and socialites who visited all the other teams. The camp had an air of nervous pressure as we saw other teams head up the mountain and heard news of daily summits from the south. *Did they know something we didn't?* I was delighted to hear that Bonita had reached the top and was safe. I knew how much she cared and how she had prepared. Knowing she had achieved her goal only furthered my desire to summit and hopefully catch up for a celebratory drink in Kathmandu. The top was made seemingly more achievable by her successful attempt.

12

HEADING INTO THE UNKNOWN

True, real inspiration and growth only comes from adversity and from challenge, from stepping away from what's comfortable and familiar and stepping out into the unknown.

Ben Saunders

When the news finally broke that we would be leaving for our summit attempt in a few days' time, the relief was palpable. Instead of being on edge and dreading whether or not we would even get our shot, people became more reflective, fearful and focused. The conversations were less jovial and trivial.

Everyone knew that we were about to go to a hostile environment that would have no qualms about shattering our dreams. Everyone knew that we would be stretched in a way many of us had not experienced before. We discussed our fears about situations we may encounter up high. We discussed whether we would have the mental strength to turn around if necessary when the summit was in sight and to what lengths we were willing to go. A few of us jested about the phrase 'summit or die', but that was really just masking our own trepidation about the impending contest in our minds.

Brendan did more interviews with people at Base Camp the day before departure.

Matt S

Pretty nervous. I know my odds of summiting are still pretty small. My biggest worry is just getting the HAPE back... getting the lungs back and there's just absolutely nothing I can do about it. I've got the meds but if it comes back to haunt me then it comes back to haunt me. There's nothing I can do about it.

I'm here. I'm still fighting. We'll see what happens.

Keith

Quite enthused and psyched up after this morning's little brief. It has got the blood pumping a bit and I'm looking forward to getting up there.

Two days ago I was worried the weather window was never going to get here and we were going to end up going home after a two-and-a-half-month camping trip without even giving it a shot.

I guess I'm worried about whether I want it enough when I get high.

As for my perspective, I wrote this in my blog:

Blog – 18 May 2010

To make the top of this mountain, there are a lot of things that have to click into place. The weather has to be good, my body has to cope with the minimal oxygen in the atmosphere etc.

That has not changed. I have acclimatised well and feel excited to try and climb to the top of the world! This mountain has plagued me every day for a number of years and I hope to grasp this opportunity with everything I've got.

Thank you for all the support – it has made a massive difference.

I will leave you with one of the most important quotes I have come across from one of the greatest American climbers.

'Getting to the top is optional. Getting down is mandatory.' – Ed Viesturs

Highlighting my apprehension of what was to come and the knowledge of the fine line between life and death, I wrote as if I knew where my priorities were. But in my mind, I was more willing to put it all on the line than I said. I certainly did not want to die but I had the innocence and arrogance of youth to believe that it would not happen to me. I was all in, my cards were on the table.

Retracing our steps to ABC was a time to process my thoughts – the calm before storm, silence before the noise. We then spent a night at ABC, loading up on as much food as possible, before beginning the summit push proper. Four days of struggle and strain in a thinning atmosphere lay ahead.

The move up the Headwall felt comfortable; this was our

third time going up the route and we each found a rhythm that worked. We moved at our own pace knowing that energy conservation would be important in the days ahead. Nobody was rushing to the front or trying to be a hero.

As we moved up, climbers passed us on their way down. Their facial expressions and manner often gave a clear indication of how their attempt had gone. The looks of anguish, pain and discomfort were evident. The effects of the weather were etched across the faces of people who had endured a lot. We wanted to know what it was like up there but few were in a mood to talk. Their staggering legs indicated they were set on one thing only and that was getting down to the safety of ABC.

The weather at the North Col was savage. Brendan's footage has him saying, 'I've never experienced wind like this before and it's only 2.20 in the afternoon.' I was with Stu and beyond my husky voice on video, the wind howl is prominent. Rips in the tent, or 'skylights' as we preferred to call them, and bent tent poles were evidence of the power of the winds. It hardly filled us with encouragement.

The monotonous and gradual North Ridge rose ahead for 500 vertical metres. Thankfully the winds subsided on the whole, which was a relief though it was still an extremely demanding day. My back was becoming excruciatingly painful. No amount of rucksack shuffling or stopping every few steps to place my hands on the ground and relieve the pressure would eradicate this. My throat was seizing up and my stomach was struggling to accept any of the food I had eaten that morning. The next few days would be about how much I could live with discomfort. This was the highest I had ever been before and every step from halfway up the North Ridge was a new step into the unknown. I climbed with Matt and Pete. We were all suffering in our own worlds but taking solace from the presence of each other. The rest of the team were spread out, each person fighting on.

From 7,500m to Camp 3 at 8,300m, there was variable snow cover and small rocky outcrops to clamber over. It was nothing technical and, thankfully, gave the mind a break after the monotony of the seemingly never-ending snow slope coming from the North Col. However, the higher altitudes were having an effect on the team.

Heather, unfortunately, did not get beyond the North Col. She had been suffering from a terrible throat and breathing issue for a few weeks and she wisely concluded that her efforts would end in vain if she continued up. It was hard to fault her efforts or determination.

At Camp 2 Jonathan sadly came to the same conclusion. He was a firefighter, a proud husband and father of two girls. His kindness and warmth drew me to him from an early stage in the expedition and I longed for him to summit. I sometimes struggled to fathom attempting the mountain with young children but he was very clear with his outlook. He said from Base Camp that, if he ever got to a position where he thought he might be in significant danger, then he was heading straight back down. When the early symptoms of HAPE set in at 7,800m, after a 12-hour day, he was true to his word. I respected him hugely for his integrity and courage.

Jonathan

The summit was so close and I felt robbed. It was now time to stick to that promise and not take a big gamble. The risks of going on were too great. Maybe when I was 20 I might have rolled the dice but life's too good and Everest does not need any more bodies lying on it. I set off down after wishing the guys well. My goggles were steamed up with the tears rolling down my cheeks. I was walking away from my dream.

I was in a tent with Keith and Pete at Camp 2 and we had all slept on supplementary oxygen which gave a noticeable boost. I found the masks restrictive and certainly uncomfortable to sleep in, but they were essential for our success. We ate what we could, but for me that was negligible. My appetite had gone, my throat was sore and I felt permanently nauseous. The effects of the altitude were brutal.

The three of us boiled as much water as we could to drink and then just lay side by side, oxygen masks on, encased in our own thoughts. It had been a 12-hour day and we were physically pretty spent. We slept as much as possible given the situation. Waking that morning at Camp 2, however, was special. The views were astounding. The tents at the North Col looked insignificant as more great peaks started to appear below our eyeline. This was why we were here – to test ourselves in this truly remarkable setting.

The move to 8,300m was agonisingly slow and arduous. Everything hurt. Everything felt uncomfortable. Each step became a considered and inelegant slog.

We were all in our down suits at this point with oxygen masks on, a team of black-and-yellow Michelin men. The summit ridge looked so detailed and real. For the first time, I could clearly make out the First, Second and Third Steps.

We had made it above 8,000m and were into what is known as the 'Death Zone' – hardly an uplifting term – the altitude at which your body is literally dying. Human life cannot be sustained at this height.

Even when I was stationary and filming Keith as he moved desperately slowly towards me, you can hear the panting on film. My heart rate remained high and I felt constantly out of breath. Each sentence was a challenge to complete. Each person's facial expression and discomfort was covered by their oxygen mask, but their pain was evident in their lack of speed and effort of movement.

Finally, the tents of Camp 3 came into view at 8,300m. The highest, and probably most unwelcoming, camp in the world. I collapsed into a tent with Matt and Pete. They had been there a few hours. We shared a pack of jelly babies and I bit into the gooey sugary block. I could not stomach anything else; I simply couldn't muster the energy. The thought was beyond me and I was shattered already. They could probably sense it although they were too good to say so. The thought of moving further up the mountain a matter of hours after arriving was disheartening. There was nothing about the thought that filled me with any optimism or hope – only impending dread.

Brendan made a short film in his tent to show how he, Ian and Matt D were feeling. The looks of exhaustion are all over their faces.

Matt D

Felt better to be honest but still alive...that's one thing. Hoping for a pretty quick recovery, a boil in the bag. That's it really.

What else can I say? Not very inspiring. Life is tough at 8,300m, there's no doubt about that.

Brendan

Everything is just a massive effort. Even just taking off your socks or moving around to get in the tent, that was an epic. The time now is 6.45 p.m. and at 10.30 p.m. we're going to be turning on the headlights and heading up to the ridge. Getting to the Second Step around sunrise. Pretty exciting to be honest but we've just got to make sure we get enough food on board and enough liquid to make it.

I also used my camera to film Matt, Pete and me. My voice is broken and a breath is required after a couple of words such is the extreme impact of the altitude.

Video Diary – 22 May 2010 9.30 p.m.

After 50 days or so, we're at high camp, about an hour and a half from setting off with Matt and Pete. Those two guys have been fucking heroes today. It has been a very, very hard day but in about 11 hours now, hopefully, we will be standing on top of the world. Fingers crossed.

13

Summit Day - 23 May 2010

Climb if you will, but remember that courage and strength are nought without prudence, and that a momentary negligence may destroy the happiness of a lifetime.

Edward Whymper

At 11 p.m. my head torch was on, my rucksack was packed and I hauled myself out of the tent and set off into the darkness. All the preparation and training over the years had led to this moment. I would like to say I felt ready for what was ahead, but truthfully, I wasn't. Matt said later, 'I remember being so focused I hadn't even considered how big a deal it was. It was just a case of cracking on.' In contrast, I saw the magnitude of what was ahead and dreaded the pain. I knew, however, that when I got going, I would just continue to trudge upwards.

Ian and Matt D hardly made it out of High Camp. Their hacking coughs and altitude sickness were too much. Soon after, Andy passed me heading in the other direction, having reached a similar conclusion. All their efforts were highly courageous and I admire them for making a tough decision.

After several hours I found myself alone and my head torch cut out. I always carried a spare but that failed to muster up any strength in the cold. It was another intense moment as darkness appeared around me except for the bobbing head torches further up the route. I felt isolated and fearful. I had a choice to make as well – turn around or continue to ascend into the unknown.

I felt strong so I continued to move up. I was now relying on the minimal exposure from the moonlight. This offered me little but vague outlines of rocks; restricting depth perception and precise footwork, it heavily reduced my speed. On a number of occasions I was unable to clip onto the fixed rope. Instead I just headed straight up and hoped that I would reconnect with the main route. I was in a heightened state of anxiety but, at the same time, felt a reckless urge to make progress.

I finally reached the Northeast Ridge and could feel the wind hitting me head-on. I had studied the route in detail and knew that, with vast drops either side of the ridge, and narrow ledges to navigate, I could not proceed in these conditions. I was forced to wait. I sat behind a rock, thus protected from the wind, and was riddled with regret. I resented that this was time wasted when I felt the willingness to move with purpose. I was regretful at my stupidity in allowing my batteries to fail. I was now reduced to waiting for two torches to approach at an agonisingly slow speed.

It was Keith and Surendra, his Sherpa. As a trio we slowly made it to the base of the First Step at around 8,550m, just as the sun had started to rise, and took a quick rest.

Suddenly, Surendra ripped his oxygen mask off. His face was panic-stricken and terrified. We tried to calm him down but he was in a frenzy. He was too frantic to explain what had happened. We tried to coerce the mask back on his face but our endeavours appeared to be futile. He then took out photos of his family from his pocket, tore them up and threw them into the atmosphere.

Nuru appeared shortly after and assessed the situation and the panic that his fellow Sherpa was in. A right hook that Mike Tyson would have been proud of surprised us all and almost knocked Surendra off his feet. The panic subsided. Nuru understood the gravity of the situation and made the decision to descend with his friend and ushered Keith and I upwards.

We unglamorously hauled ourselves up the First Step. We were precise with our crampon movement but our lethargic efforts appeared to be in slow motion. We managed to clamber over the lip and thankfully that 20m obstacle was now behind us.

Second Step, Third Step, summit slopes, summit. I knew what was ahead but just had to keep putting one foot in front of the other.

At the top of the First Step, Keith looked at me inquisitively and asked what our plan was with this impending weather. In the past 30 minutes, the sun had risen and the darkness had been replaced by clear blue skies and a shimmering orange glow across the peaks far below us. I was perplexed by the question but, again, he insisted that we should be wary of the clouds overhead.

Keith

As daylight came over, I went from being able to see the curvature of the earth, within half an hour or so, to being able to see 10 or 20 metres. I assumed it was the weather coming in but, having spoken to the one person I could see within 10 metres of me, he said it was gin-clear and he could see forever. I checked my goggles, rubbed my eyes and made the decision to turn around.

Keith realised his corneas had begun to freeze, a common but unpredictable issue at high altitude, and made the tough choice to turn around. His priorities, as an experienced Army Officer, switched immediately from the focus of summiting Everest. It was an immensely wise and mature decision.

I was vulnerable and alone once again. When dissecting the route on the Northeast Ridge of Everest, it is impossible to get a sense of what it will feel like to be there. Having such an enormous drop looming beneath the precarious ledges you balance on makes it an extremely daunting experience. It is not the kind of nauseating exposure like being halfway up a vertical rock climb but, combined with the extreme exhaustion, it meant the psychological hurdles to overcome were as profound as the physical ones.

As I dragged my way along the fixed rope, I could see it trying to wrestle free from the piton attaching it to the rock further ahead. I continued to slide my jumar forward in the knowledge that it would force my body to follow.

It takes years to become an expert at using crampons on rock. Having faith in the one inch of metal meticulously placed in a rivet on a rock face is something I was never truly at ease with. The traversing sections along the narrow ridge between the First and Second Steps exposed us to the depths below and the knowledge that a single mistake could be our last. Having successfully navigated that section, I changed my oxygen bottle at Mushroom Rock and proceeded onto the fabled Second Step.

To my surprise, I came across two stationary teammates. Brian, the Lone Wolf, was sitting with Mark. Brian said he was still going up but Mark was on his way down and said it was not to be. I used the opportunity to sit down, rest and increase the flow of oxygen before I headed up.

I was good to go but Brian asked for more time, which I gratefully gave him in the knowledge of what was to come. I eventually became restless and fumbled my way past. Brian hardly responded. Mark and I urged him up but he had become increasingly altitude sick, slightly delirious and was slurring his words. He could not remember our names, started to have a conversation with his rucksack as though it were a human being and could not remember how to put it on.

Mark and I helped him up and Mark assured me that he, with the assistance of two descending Sherpas from another team, could safely descend with Brian while I kept going.

In terms of my attempt, it was more time lost but I edged on in my insular world of focus. I felt compelled not to turn around. I cannot explain what it was but I was convinced that I had to keep going.

Onto the Second Step. A Chinese team had left a ladder here from their attempt in 1975, enabling the successful passage of climbers that have made it since. I could only imagine what George Mallory must have felt as he came to the base of this 40m obstacle. Looking at it through a telescope is one thing but to be at the base of it is quite another. I had analysed every picture and watched every clip I could. Yet, standing there in full sunlight I felt intimidated. I inelegantly grabbed a handful of fixed ropes, new and old, and scratched my crampons up the first section.

My heart was pounding due to fear, the exposure and physical exertion. My lungs cried out for more air, thirsty for any oxygen they could find. I removed my mask out of curiosity and desperation to see if it was restricting my flow of oxygen. I pleaded for something to give but got nothing back so replaced the mask and calmed myself as much as possible.

Don't look down, don't look down, I kept telling myself. Despite people's perception, I feel uneasy with heights and uncomfortable in highly exposed situations. I try to rationalise it, see the fear as entirely illogical and make precise decisions to ensure my safety. Attached to one of the ropes I was about to clip onto was the body of a climber. Lying at the bottom of the Second Step, at 8,610m, he wore the same boots as me and a similar down suit. I'd been warned it was there but was still utterly stunned and genuinely scared for my life.

It was the first body I had ever seen. My legs wobbled and shook uncontrollably as my mind raced. I kept saying to myself, *I don't want to end up like that. I don't want to be in that position.*

I tried to adjust my focus upwards instead of down. I stepped away from this ledge and towards the ladder. I was out of breath. My heart was pounding hard and my legs unstable. I reflected for a moment, considering my options, as two climbers descended the ladder. Then I clipped on and made the choice to keep going. One rung at a time before I hauled myself to the top and kept moving.

Much to my surprise, I then encountered Stephen sitting down. He cut a frustrated figure and claimed he'd been given two empty oxygen bottles so could not make the summit. I remained with him partly to calm myself but also to keep him company. We waited until Brendan joined us, having made the top, and I left Stephen with him and continued on in a fatigued daze. Stu passed me about 10 minutes later, assessed my state, reminded me of our turn-around time and let me crack on.

I was scared, alone, aged only 21 and without a radio. *What was I doing?*

Only 150m to go. I could see the Third Step now; I could see the summit slopes. The end was in sight. Each step required me to dig deep into my reserves. Everything was telling me to stop. I had navigated my way through the chaos below and was now left with the chaos in my own head.

I was searching for something to allow me to go beyond

what my body and mind thought possible. I was searching for *sisu*. Searching for that spirit within to keep each foot moving forward. *Sisu* is the unseen resolve within us, that motivation within, and at that moment I needed it more than ever. Each step was one step closer to the top. Nobody could tell me to stop now. I had to keep moving.

I then encountered Max and Sherpa Sonam, who told me it was about four hours to the summit, despite the minimal amount of altitude I needed to gain. It was 9 a.m. and it dawned on me that my turnaround time of 11 a.m. was not achievable. I knew the risks that lay ahead as a solo and relatively inexperienced climber. I knew deep down that my energy resources were fairly depleted. Equally, I had obsessed about reaching the summit of Everest for over three years and this was my only chance. Stick or twist. Should I, in Kipling's words, 'risk it on one turn of pitch-and-toss' or give up?

I sat down, gazed vacantly across the Tibetan plateau that lay sprawling beneath me, looked up at the summit and knew that it was over at 8,700m, within 150m of the summit of Everest.

My willpower was sapped from within me. My body had been clinging on, my mind denying it the chance to yield to the pain. As Max and I moved slowly downhill, the summit focus now removed, my mind began to crumble. I could not ignore the searing pain shooting through my back. My throat had seized and regular coughing of blood became unavoidable. The distraction mechanisms I had often used to detach myself from the discomfort of a situation became futile and the failings, physical and human, were very real.

The increasingly vague expedition blog was leaving my

family and friends hugely uncertain as to what was happening. I had a group of mates at St Andrews waiting up until the early hours with a bottle of champagne at the ready and Klara was in constant communication with my sisters and parents. The last information they had was that I was alone and heading for the summit.

Adventure Peaks Everest Blog – 23 May 2010 8.35 a.m.

No news for definite in the last few hours.

It is understood, however (not confirmed) that a number of team members turned round between 8,600–8,700m.

Geordie was the last person who may have made the summit before the turnaround time. We await news.

Adventure Peaks Everest Blog – 23 May 2010 11 a.m.

Things are not great in Camp 3 and they have decided to stay the night there. There are eight Sherpas at Camp 3 to assist Stu to assist everyone down tomorrow.

The weather up there right now looks terrible and Matt D confirmed that conditions were extremely challenging.

Everything is really broken up and unclear.

I forced myself to keep moving for as long as possible but would regularly come to a halt and slump to the ground in moments of despair and self-doubt. Max had given me a few throat sweets which provided temporary relief – but then pain came shooting back at me with full force.

In Mum's words, 'We all stayed up all night because he was supposed to be there by midnight or the early hours (UK time). But there was no real word of where he was so we sort of panicked for a bit and then realised we couldn't panic, that there was nothing we could do.'

Dad described the experience from a parental perspective as, 'Particularly poignant and harrowing.' I cannot truly comprehend what was going through their heads.

I just wanted it to end. To be at Base Camp. My dream was over.

14

It's Not Over – The Descent

The mountains will always be there. The trick is to make sure you are too.

Hervey Voge

Sisu is not momentary courage, but the ability to sustain that courage. According to expert Emilia Lahti, 'It is the enigmatic power that enables individuals to push through significant hardship.' *Sisu* begins where resilience and perseverance end. It is that extra gear of psychological strength. It is pushing through when you're seemingly at your maximum capacity.

This was a time when again I was searching deeply for *sisu*. I had to find more strength and courage from somewhere. I knew I had to get down. I had to survive.

The obsessive urge to get to the top had obviously dissipated. It had been replaced with a deep desire to make it back alive. My legs were somehow moving but my mind was all over the place. Finally, I got back to High Camp, momentary respite at least. Our tent was being used to shelter Brian who was apparently not doing well.

Matt

At 8,300m we were still vulnerable to the altitude, especially in our current physical condition. Succumbing to the tiredness and spending the night at Camp 3 without oxygen could have been fatal. We were greeted by Geordie. He looked in a bad way, exhausted, frost-nipped/sunburnt face and still struggling to talk. He told us he hadn't managed to make the summit. I was gutted for him, we both were.

I took a video at High Camp with Matt and Pete who had both just summited Everest, asking them how they felt. 'Pretty fucking shagged if I'm honest mate...very tired. Yep, very tired.' Our weary demeanour and hoarse voices say more than the words.

We left High Camp and headed down the mountain as darkness began to set in. We had left it quite late but just hoped to make it down to Camp 2 and rest.

It was now pitch black, snowing and bitterly cold. We were exhausted, having not slept or eaten much in 72 hours. We struggled to find our tent. Pete and I had continued 20m down the hill when Matt yelled from above that he had located it. The battle to make that pitiful ascent was formidable. We were running on empty. We just about summoned up enough energy to boil a bit of water each. Then, still in our down suits, we passed out.

Our tent shook violently at 6 a.m. and a Nepalese voice told us in no uncertain terms that we needed to get moving. We probably could have continued to sleep long into the day. Our oxygen bottles had run out so our bodies were in serious oxygen and calorific depletion.

It seemed to take an age to get ready as three of us shuffled around in a total daze. We made unbelievably slow progress. The fatigue was so deep but the power of moving as a group was enough to keep us going somehow. We were all in serious need of *sisu* from somewhere, our energy levels running dangerously low.

We reached the top of the snow slope at 7,500m and it was a total whiteout. Any visible skin was pelted with horizontal daggers of snow. The deep powder was draining us even more and it was not an environment to hang around in so improvisation was required. In a rare wave of humour and clarity, assisted by deep exhaustion, we adopted a unique three-man bobsled position, which increased our progress exponentially. We would crash into each snow picket, unclip, secure ourselves again and continue. Thankfully the pickets were strong enough and the lines slack enough to allow this while the deep snow prevented us picking up too much momentum. I have loved the film *Cool Runnings* since I was a child so felt pleased to be able to re-enact it in such an extraordinary location. The next 400m were probably the most fun we had on the mountain.

We thought, having got to the North Col, that a routine descent of the Headwall was all that was required and we could collapse into camp. The Sherpas were tentatively using walking poles to check the stability of the ground before moving across it. The glacier was clearly in a precarious state and the crevasse risk was enormous. We followed their lead and cautiously made progress, edging our way around the eerie chasms. Visibility was now reduced to a matter of metres and their pace ensured we lost our Sherpa lead without trace of their route. Our hypoxic state made our choices significantly harder.

Pete was a few metres ahead but I then looked around after I heard a crack and Matt was suddenly up to his shoulders. I called for Pete but he couldn't hear and I had to wait for him to return before doing anything.

Pete

Peering through the blizzard, my eyes suddenly caught sight of Geordie sitting down on the rocky ridge. Scanning further around I saw that Matt's shoulders and head were protruding out of the ground...Bollocks. He was in a crevasse. Managing to cautiously make my way over to him, I found Matt in a frantic state. I could see in his eyes he was deeply worried that we wouldn't be able to get him out.

After checking that he hadn't broken anything, we worked out a recovery method. We had to reduce the weight near him in case the surface was unstable and Pete bravely lay himself next to his mate to work out a plan.

I held a safety line attached from my harness to Pete's and allowed him to edge over the lip. Slowly he chipped away at the ice around Matt's foot and together they hauled themselves back to where I was where we fell in a heap in silent reflection. It was a lucky escape and we all knew it.

As we reached the base of the Headwall the clouds parted and we were welcomed by blue skies. Finally, though none of us said anything for fear of cursing it, we all believed we would make it back in one piece.

We dumped our crampons, ice axes and rucksacks outside the mess tent and looked at each other – seeing, beyond the fraught expressions on our faces, deep within. We knew we were lucky to make it back alive.

People were a little shocked at the state of us when we came through the door. I looked and felt truly awful. My face had been assaulted by vicious winds, sunburn, extreme cold and exposure to high altitude. I was relieved to see everyone alive and well but emotionally, physically and mentally I was absolutely broken. I had given everything I had.

We went to our tents and collapsed, still in our down suits before finally reaching the deep sleep our bodies and minds so dearly craved. It had been the hardest and most intense day of my life.

The Inquest Begins

It is through failure that we experience our limitations. And it is for that reason that failure is a more powerful experience than success.

Reinhold Messner

One of our leaders, Matt D, said before we went for our summit attempt, 'I dare say there's going to be some stories to tell.' I had read so many tales of epic mountaineering feats from all over the world, with horrendous injuries and fatalities. Thank God, and it is still beyond me how, but nobody on our team did die. Still, it would take a long time for us to come to terms with what had happened. Everyone wanted to know how only four of the 12 guys that started out on summit day had made the top.

Stephen and Josh, in particular, felt hard done by. Due to

equipment and oxygen failures, their attempts had been scuppered. They went round camp in delirium trying to find Sherpas to take them back up the mountain. They had not even seen the forecast but were insistent, determined not to accept failure.

I half-heartedly offered myself up for a second attempt. They probably knew I was lying to myself, but it added weight to the argument that it was not just the two of them. One look in the mirror would have been enough for me to realise I was not capable of making another effort. The mind was vaguely willing but the body was in total disarray.

None of the Sherpas, from our team or others, were willing to go back up. They were wary about the weather and equally fatigued; they had also been pushed hard. They reflected on their religious principles and believed that the Gods were not looking kindly on the mountain, so it would not be right to head back up. Josh and Stephen struggled to comprehend this rationale but had no choice but to accept it. For the Sherpas, the high mountains represent more than just an objective to achieve – they have spiritual significance. This had been illustrated by Surendra's refusal to accept the help Keith and I tried to give him before the First Step. From their perspective, the 2010 climbing season was over.

I just wanted to head down to Base Camp and gather my thoughts, away from the chaos of the higher slopes. The forecast had begun to turn grim and even with their best efforts, a summit attempt would not have been possible. We were forced to turn our backs to the mountain.

Before I left ABC I took a film that truly represented how I felt. It shows the brutality of the weather on my face, the rawness of my throat, and the disenchantment.

Video Diary – 26 May 2010

The tents here at ABC are being taken down and it looks like my Everest 2010 dream is over, sadly. I did my very best but it's just not to be.

The mountain took more out of me than I ever anticipated but as the Guinness advert says...the best things come to those who wait.

When we all got down to Base Camp we could finally process what had happened in the comfort of the oxygen-rich air and decent food. Jonathan and Brian had already been evacuated to Kathmandu for their extreme altitude sickness. I felt for Jonathan, he was a good man, and I knew he had left for his own safety; but I had lost respect for Brian, the Lone Wolf.

I was angry at him and wanted to know what the hell was going on in his head when I encountered him at the bottom of the Second Step or why he had even continued up in that state. In my mind to compromise other people's safety, as well as their summit ambitions, was extremely misjudged and selfish. A doctor by trade, and a father, I would have expected him to be more considerate of others, but mountains can strip away the very fabric of one's true character. Human beings are like teabags – you only know how strong they are when you put them in hot water.

Brian was immensely fortunate to survive. After I left him at the Second Step, he descended as far as the Exit Cracks and sat down. He was found hours later lying down off the main route. He was suffering from severe altitude sickness and HACE. It required Stu to short-rope him down to High Camp. There he received more support, before mustering enough energy to stumble down the mountain with Sherpas. I reflected on my decision to continue upwards at the Second Step and weighed up whether I did the right thing. Should the worst have happened, I would certainly have felt an element of responsibility and guilt. *Was I the Priest and Levite that had walked on by? Could I have done more to help? What if he had died?* I still don't know the answer.

Josh, who had made it down to ABC in reasonable condition after he turned around, said, 'Listening to the radio communication on the mountain was serious. How everyone made it back safely given their condition was down to fortune more than judgement.' He was right. Circumstances could have slightly altered and instead of blogs to write and flights to change, it could very conceivably have been a call to a distraught parent or wife, whose life would be changed forever.

My other teammates were thoughtful about the decisions they made but took comfort they made the right call given their condition. They had done their best. Stephen and Josh were still frustrated at the situation, but knew that their efforts were commendable, even if fate left the summit out of their reach. Mark was regretful. Despite not being particularly strong during the course of the expedition, he made good time on summit day and should have made the top. He had got to the awkward traverse on the Second Step and been too unnerved to continue; it was gnawing away at him.

Discussions about what could have been done differently were already underway and Stu was quietly pondering how events had transpired. His progress on summit day had been fairly smooth. Some people questioned why he, as a two-time summiteer and team leader, was out of touch with the main body of his climbers as well as having a Sherpa alongside him, but I was undecided on that matter.

In Brendan's words, 'One thing is for sure. Summit or no summit, we all shared an epic adventure that will forever change our lives.'

The summiteers were all spent in terms of energy but relieved to have successfully made the top. The spectrum of feelings, however, brought tension to the group. We drove out of Base Camp and my body felt hollow as the majestic beauty of Everest slowly disappeared from view to a mere speck in the distance. So tantalisingly close and yet so very far.

When we finally returned to Kathmandu in the following few days, we could begin to unwind properly. I remember getting in the shower and cleansing my frayed skin. I then sat down with the water falling on me and was overcome with sadness.

I was emotionally overdrawn. I had done everything I could, but instead of celebrating I was sitting alone in a shower and crying.

The physicality, the self-imposed pressure, the harsh exposure to life. I was still young and it had all been too much for me.

I did eventually go out into town with Matt, Pete, Brendan and Max. I tried, as a friend, to share their joy and success but it was a struggle. I also felt bad for them in a way as they could not truly share their accomplishment. We all so craved to be in their position but the mixed emotions were clear on our faces.

In the bars in Kathmandu, there was physical evidence of the hardship and suffering that people had put themselves through. Bandaged hands, charred cheekbones and weathered noses were dotted about. Although each person probably had a hell of a story to tell, that could wait for another time.

I was done with Nepal and done with Everest at that point. I just wanted to get home and see my family and girlfriend. I missed them more now than ever. I knew they would be worried and I just wanted to hug them and say I loved them all.

I wrote this blog, and a blow-by-blow account of my summit day, from Kathmandu. Freddie had already updated my website saying I had not made the summit but there had been little news since. It was a mature perspective but not entirely accurate. I don't think I could properly convey my true sentiments for a while yet and used the mask of a carefully written blog to paper over how I really felt.

Blog – 27 May 2010

As for the top – some of my closest friends from the expedition did summit and I am delighted for them. Very few people deserve it more.

I am writing this now from Kathmandu, pretty reflective, and contemplating what happened and what I could have done differently.

I take solace in knowing that I gave all I could, and a lot more, to achieve the summit. On summit day itself, it would have taken an extremely cold man to not stop and help when I did and I know that I made the right choices at the right time. Somebody else's life is more important than the summit of Everest but I agree; it is a shame I had to experience that.

Thank you for following my progress, I hope you all know I gave one million percent to get to the top and will, I'm sure, get there in the coming years!

On the plane from Kathmandu to London, the captain came over the tannoy and announced, 'If you look to your right now, you will see Mount Everest, the highest mountain in the world.' I closed my eyes and put my head back. I could not bring myself to look at the mountain that had shattered my dreams.

The North Face of Everest. A seemingly unattainable photo on my wall for so many years.

Traversing that North Face at 8,800m with Dorje on 26 May 2011. I knew the summit was close.

Summit of Aconcagua. A real learning curve aged 18 but thankfully a successful venture.

Heading up Kilimanjaro with Basha. With little time to prepare, my Kili trip was quite rash, and far from recommended, but taught me a lot.

Trekking near Elbrus in August 2009. The mountain represented the end of an intense 18 months before I headed off to St Andrews.

With Heidi at the summit of Denali.
A superb guide but more than that, a hugely genuine and kind woman.

Clockwise: Josh, myself, Keith, Pete and
Matt at Base Camp in 2010

Heading into the Death Zone at 8,000m
on Everest in 2010.

Moving to High Camp at 8,300m.
Painfully slow progress at that altitude
but getting there one step at a time.

Descending from 7,800m with Matt and
Pete. Real *sisu* conditions with terrible
weather and tired bodies. © Pete Sunnocks

The photo that Pete took 150m from the summit.
It plagued my thoughts day after day knowing how close I got. © Pete Sunnocks

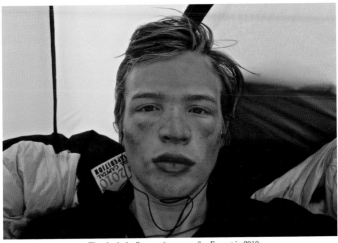

The physical toll was quite severe after Everest in 2010.
The other battle was going on unseen and took longer to recover from.

Getting my Seven Summits ambition back on track in Antarctica in December 2010.

Clockwise:
Approaching the summit of Carstensz Pyramid after a spectacular rock climb.
Trekking through the jungles of Western Papua.
David with some of the wonderful children we met at Suanggama.
One of The Dani Tribe - our amazing porters during the expedition.

Acclimatising in Nepal in 2011. You can just see the clouds whipping off the summit of Everest in the background.

Sherpa Dorje Khatri. An amazing man who kept his word after he promised to take me to the top of the world with him.

Enjoying a break on Everest in 2011. It wasn't all hardship and suffering.

Looking down along the Northeast Ridge of Everest from the Third Step. © Chris Szymiec

26 May 2011 6.30 a.m. Summit of Mount Everest.
Everything I dreamed of and more.

Introspection

If you are depressed, you are living in the past. If you are anxious, you are living in the future. If you are at peace, you are living in the present.

Lao Tzu

I had to fight back the tears as I came through the doors at Heathrow. I wanted to be the Geordie Stewart from the blog who conveyed such maturity and wisdom. I wanted to keep the real one, the one beleaguered by his own doubts, concealed from view.

Klara shrieked as she bounded towards me and gave me a hug. Holding her gave me a reprieve from my emotional anguish. Seeing my family there, feeling their love and compassion, was indescribable. They were overjoyed to see me but their celebrations were at my presence rather than my achievements. I was incredibly fortunate to possess that non-judgmental love in my life.

The jubilation of Matt and Pete's welcome party contrasted with the support of mine. I said farewell to them. What we had experienced covered the whole spectrum of human emotion. We did not know where our paths would head but we had been on an incomparable journey that could not be erased from our memories.

The initial buzz of being back at home wore off quite soon. Their empathy was unrivalled but although seeing Klara and my family was precious, my head was in a different place. I felt especially bad for Klara. I do not think I could fully reciprocate the love she gave after I returned. I had huge amounts of love for her and missed her physically and emotionally, both of which were amazing to reconnect with, but really I just wanted to be with my own thoughts.

Back at home, having dreamt of mowing the lawn and relaxing with a gin and tonic in the British sunshine, I felt uninspired.

I believed in the words I'd written but my blog did not scratch the surface of what was actually happening. It represented the tip of an emotional iceberg. I wanted to keep the truth below the surface and out of sight.

According to Lao Tzu's definition, 'If you are depressed, you are living in the past.' That's where my head was: living in what had gone before. I was depressed.

Reading my teammates' accounts of their attempts, successful or otherwise, I found it amazing how people's versions differed from the reality. Like mine, the blogs were not always completely honest and often gave a rose-tinted insight into what the person was actually feeling. Maybe sharing the full story would almost be too much to accept. Josh and Keith were, however, honest and reflective in how they viewed their attempts.

Josh

A trip like that makes you appreciate the small things in life. You realise you are in a difficult environment and you've got to be really polarised and clear in the decisions you make.

The way we did it was, for me, unquestionably the hardest thing I've ever done. We were fortunate to come out of it alive with the incidents that occurred and six people on the north side of the mountain died this year. It is a very risky place that puts life into perspective.

When you are a young man, you want to take on the world and then with age you mellow and recognise other things are increasingly important in life.

In light of the above, I'm sure that some find this challenge easier than others but for us and the way we did it, it was indeed the ultimate test of resolve, fortitude and patience.

Keith

You begin to justify to yourself that actually there was nothing more we could have done. That actually on that day, you need a lot of things to go right and we were lacking some so we became content with how it went even if there is regret.

This is the blog that I hoped I'd never have to write. Despite the

massive disappointment of not having achieved our ultimate
goal, and the fact that we were so close, on reflection, the whole
experience has been exceptional, and provided a vehicle to test
ourselves to the very limit.

They appeared to have reached the psychological state I craved – contentment. Perhaps that came from age, experience or having represented your country at the highest level. They knew they had given it their best shot and could move on with their life. I, however, could not.

In his poem If – as good an approach to life as I have seen – Rudyard Kipling says,

> *'If you can meet with Triumph and Disaster*
> *And treat those two impostors just the same...'*

I was unable to do that.

I talked on the phone to Josh while aimlessly walking around my garden barefoot. He spoke with clarity about the conclusions he had reached. He said he knew he could summit, so what was the point of going back for the final 150m? For me, it was all about those 150m. I could not fathom how that was not the case with him. I was jealous of the peace in his mind.

I spent my days in a deck chair in the garden. If the sun was shining, whatever time of day, morning or evening, I would usually be sitting alone with a Budweiser in one hand and a cigarette in the other.

It appeared an image of calm but it wasn't. It was discontent.

Beneath the screen of my sunglasses was a heavy feeling of loneliness, regret and failure. I craved mental silence but, instead, there was loud noise.

I watched Matt and Pete's summit video and there was a photo they had taken at sunrise somewhere between the Second and Third Steps, near where I had turned around. I set it as the background to my phone and laptop. It plagued my thoughts. The summit slopes were so near. The summit so agonisingly close. I went to sleep with the image in my head. I woke up and it was still there – inescapable. I replayed the day again and again in my head wondering what I could have done differently.

Why didn't I eat properly at High Camp to give myself more energy?
Why didn't I set off earlier?
Why did I buy that head torch?
Why did I even wait for Brian? He would never have waited for me.
Why did I wait with Stephen? There was nothing I could help him with.
Why did I turn around when I spoke to Max?
Why the fuck didn't I just carry on, summit and then rely on my will to live to get me back down again?
Why didn't I summit?

My poor mother did the best she could to cook meals and care. She said in an interview, 'He was pretty drained of energy; pretty drained of emotion too to be quite honest.' Poor Klara did the best she could by showing love and tenderness. I cut people off who tried to help. I felt guilty but could not see beyond my blinkered perspective.

Days turned into weeks, and well into the summer months, I still isolated myself from real conversations and people around me. I hardly saw friends despite their willingness to try. I ignored the media who wanted to know what had happened. I felt depressed, unmotivated and alone.

17

LOOKING AHEAD

My great concern is not whether you have failed, but whether you are content with your failure.

Abraham Lincoln

The great Norwegian explorer and philosopher, Erling Kagge, is a strong advocate for the power of silence. In the days of iPhones and social media, the quest for peace can be a struggle, but it is through calm that we find clarity. The process of pausing and reflecting is what gives us a greater understanding of self and what brings each of us joy. He says, 'Through silence, you start to get answers to some questions that you didn't even know you had been asking yourself.'

In the period post-Everest, I used silence to help me find the peace I was seeking. Long walks and sitting alone in the garden provided enough harmony to allow my mind to find comfort. Silence can be a meditative experience – not necessarily a focused period of yoga or meditation, but giving myself the opportunity to just be absorbed by my own thoughts away from the stresses of life was something crucial to my own wellbeing.

One thing I will forever be grateful for is the kindness that others showed me. While struggling to come to terms with what had happened, on an almost daily basis I received letters, emails and messages from people whose opinions I valued. I probably didn't realise it at the time but, looking back, this is what began to reveal more of the iceberg. I was allowing myself to be content.

The letters below are words and sentiments from people that I cared about and who cared about me. It showed the level of support I had – success or failure – which helped me get out of the cloud of self-pity that I was enveloped in.

> *The courage you so obviously showed in making those decisions and following your convictions shows a great humility and selflessness. None of us can begin to imagine what you went through or how you felt.*
>
> *I just wanted you to know that we are all so proud of you.*

> *By the sound of it, you certainly did the right thing and could have asked no more of yourself: well done. To the dispassionate observer, the way you dealt with the tribulations of the climb is a triumph as great as reaching the summit. That said, someday I hope you realise your dream.*

From the bottom of ours hearts, well done!

Perhaps I misinterpreted your disappointment at the final outcome but I couldn't help but wonder if you don't fully comprehend the significance of what you've achieved. To have forced your nerve and sinew to accept your will in the most inhospitable of conditions; to have overcome your understandable fear; to have sacrificed the final 150m for the greater good, all showed a physical and moral courage that is incomprehensible to the rest of us.

A triumph it most certainly was.

———

There was no sudden awakening or moment of enlightenment but gradually I started to live with my decisions. I had begun the healing process of acceptance and could think about moving on.

Sisu is not just about physical courage or endeavour. *Sisu* is also about overcoming adversity, struggling through personal difficulty and finding contentment. My search for *sisu* was not simply about hardship over 8,000m. It was not just about finding deep physical reserves and not giving up. It was also about finding peace within. Peace with the decisions I'd made and the direction of my moral compass. *Sisu* was about looking into the mirror at a time of disquiet and being comfortable with the reflection.

Some, like Josh and Keith, got there soon after returning to the UK and moved to the next stage of their life. I did not have their perspective to see the bigger picture. Everest had dominated my thoughts for over three years and only after the intensely emotional phase of self-reflection could I find some sort of clarity. I had worked incredibly hard just to get to Base Camp, let alone 8,700m above sea level, and was proud of that. That is not to say I concluded the desire to stand on the summit of Everest was a worthless one – far from it.

Perhaps I needed time to acknowledge how exhausted I was on the descent and how fortunate we were to make it back safely. I still believed that if I had continued up then I would have made the final 150m in a few hours. However, a solo descent at my age, with the levels of exhaustion I had, could well have been beyond me. That would have been at least another five hours at over 8,700m with limited oxygen, no communication and no contingency plan in terms of rescue if something had happened. To have continued up would have meant trying to get down the three Steps in the darkness as the winds picked up on the Northeast Ridge. Anything could have happened.

By objectively analysing the circumstances, I managed to re-evaluate the decisions I made and a curtain lifted to reveal a wider understanding of the incidents that took place. This allowed me to be more restful with my decision to turn my back on the summit as I knew deep down it had been the right thing to do.

I spoke to Stu at Adventure Peaks. He had been with me on the day and understood the situation. We discussed what went wrong both for me personally and collectively. As a team, we compiled a list of improvement points for the following year and Stu reckoned they were fair and could be implemented.

The call ended and I decided to make another commitment:

to attempt Everest again the following year. However, I wanted to make it the final mountain of my Seven Summits attempt after successfully climbing Vinson in Antarctica and Carstensz Pyramid in Indonesia. A busy nine months lay ahead.

I had a new focus and a new(ish) dream!

I then made another commitment. I would have to take a year out of St Andrews to make this happen. Two months on Everest and two months on Vinson and Carstensz, on top of the fundraising and training made it unmanageable. I had to throw all my eggs into one Everest-shaped basket.

I stayed with a friend in Chamonix to get my head back in the game. I wanted to climb again for the love of it. My body had not recovered properly but it did not matter; I was outside in nature. This was where I was happiest and most at one with the world.

I summited the Matterhorn, an iconic and stunning mountain, near Zermatt. I needed to reach the top of a big mountain to rebuild my confidence and the Matterhorn was the perfect medicine. I also met up with Brendan, a teammate from Everest, had some beers and sang some Bob Dylan songs back at his flat. It was great to reflect on what had happened, laugh at characters we'd encountered along the way and brainstorm about what was ahead. He was a great sounding board and fully behind my plans for 2011. I have always found that vocalising a plan to other people is one certain way to get things going. The wheels were now in motion.

18

VINSON MASSIF

4,892m / 16,050ft

Optimism, pessimism, fuck that – we're going to make it happen. As God is my bloody witness, I'm hell-bent on making it work.

Elon Musk

With new-found zest and hope, I set to work. Having spoken to my 2010 team of Dad and Freddie, we arranged a meeting to formulate a plan. This time, Freddie and I felt much more comfortable with what was required and how we would go about the task. We had made mistakes for Everest 2010 in terms of marketing, media awareness and sponsorship proposals. Our 'throw enough mud at the wall and some of it will stick' approach had fortunately worked out. For the completion of the Seven Summits, however, the costs were vastly increased but, equally, so was the potential media exposure at the end.

The battle on the mountain had become a battle on the laptop and a battle of sales. It was about lateral thinking, relentless research, belligerence and good fortune. I knew it would be a rocky road ahead but we didn't have a choice.

This was now a business and our job was to raise enough sponsorship for three expeditions. We were great mates who worked well together. We were willing to bounce ideas around, willing to drive each other up the wall; there was a large amount of mutual respect. That, combined with Golden Virginia tobacco, Fifa and coffee, seemed to head us off in the right direction.

It was a different set of skills to what was required on the mountain but that in itself was a challenge I wanted to excel at. I knew there were people out there who would benefit from being part of the project. It was just about finding them.

Finding sponsors was extremely tough regardless of how persistent and creative we were being. The process some-times felt truly futile.

We collated beautiful sponsorship packs. I called and called and called. I then I emailed and emailed and emailed. I had spreadsheets galore of companies and their personnel profiles, and each time would prepare a glorious 'elevator pitch' as to why *they* should sponsor Geordie Stewart Seven Summits. I had to convince myself that every time I picked up the phone was going to be *the* conversation that mattered.

If I was persistent enough to get through to the person I wanted to speak to, often using some elaborate corporate business meeting as a bluff on the phone, I would get asked to email my proposal through; and then nothing. In fact, it got to the stage where I would be delighted even to get a response from letters or emails. But receiving these sorts of emails time and time again started to wear a little thin.

> *Thank you for your email. We have forwarded your message on to the relevant department and they will be in contact should they wish to discuss this further with you.*
>
> *I do hope this helps, and the best of luck with your expedition!*

Or

> *Unfortunately, due to a number of other sponsorship commitments, we are not in a position to support your challenge.*
>
> *However, I wish you the very best in your endeavours.*

In 2011 I decided I wanted to climb in aid of the Royal National Lifeboat Institution (RNLI), the charity that saves lives at sea. The RNLI provides a 24-hour rescue service across the shores of the UK and the Republic of Ireland, helping save the lives of more than 400 people per year (and almost 150,000 since its inception in 1824). My family have supported it ever since my grandfather was rescued by them on two separate occasions after he was shot down in a Spitfire in World War II. I believed in the cause and it served as extra motivation to try to raise as much money as I could.

The first person to back us to enable the expedition to Antarctica was Philip Magor of Williamson Tea, in the form of their Lifeboat Tea branch. That Lifeboat Tea actively supported the RNLI and donated a percentage of every sale to the charity tied in perfectly.

Also on board was Knight Frank Estate Agents. Andrew Rome from Knight Frank was hugely supportive of the project when he heard about it and I was fortunate that his persuasive traits did the trick. As it transpired, it was another excellent relationship that hugely benefitted both parties.

As with S.W. Mitchell Capital for Everest 2010, the faith that Andrew and Philip showed was amazing and facilitated the journey's unfolding. I was enormously grateful and wanted to repay that faith the best I could.

Antarctica has always been a place for the intrepid explorer. It is a place where humans have been tested to their limits and often struggled on to a bitter and lonely end. I spent my childhood listening to stories from my dad about Shackleton's epic rescue of his men and Amundsen cruelly pipping Captain Scott to the South Pole. Scott's painfully honest accounts on his return from the Pole, during which journey he and his four teammates died, have long resonated with me as true examples of courage and stoicism.

We have gone downhill a good deal since I wrote. Poor Titus

Oates has gone – he was in a bad state – the rest of us keep going and imagine we have a chance to get through but the cold weather doesn't let up at all – we are now only 20 miles from a depot but we have very little food or fuel. It is not easy to write because of the cold – 70 degrees below zero and nothing but the shelter of our tent.

Since writing the above we have got to within 11 miles of our depot with one hot meal and two days' cold food and we should have got through but have been held for four days by a frightful storm – I think the best chance has gone.

I loved tales of Fridtjof Nansen (a former Rector at St Andrews), Erling Kagge and Sir Ranulph Fiennes – men who just headed off into this barren wilderness, with a masochistic urge to cover vast landscapes for greater distances or more consecutive days or with less support than the previous person.

I loved the loneliness and solitude that these explorers experienced. The sense of peace versus the lone struggle against your mind and nature.

I was neither going solo nor was I exploring new territory but I was heading to the coldest, driest, highest and windiest continent on earth.

After a maze of flights to Punta Arenas, the small town on the southern tip of Chile, our team of four Brits was ready to board a former Russian cargo plane, an Ilyushin Il-76, to Antarctica. The flight in a rickety old machine was hardly luxurious travel but it served a purpose and we kept our down jackets and cold weather boots nearby for arrival.

Even getting a flight at all was fortunate. I had only just

covered the costs of the expedition through my sponsorship, so any delay in Chile would have left me in a precarious position. It was commonplace for teams to be delayed days and even weeks as the variable weather would not allow the plane to fly.

On board were people from all over the globe with different Antarctic aspirations. There were Russian climbers going to Vinson, a Korean team trying to cross the continent using nothing but solar energy to power their Ski-Doos and Australians wishing to ski the last degree to the South Pole.

Unique places attract unique people.

Since I can remember I had thought of going to this remarkable continent, but it always appeared improbable. I strained to look out the window and see what it was actually like. We had all seen pictures of the vast swathes of whiteness but I couldn't wait to experience that in real life. As soon as the plane thudded against the ice runway, a rarity in itself, a frozen blast powered through the cabin and we, in turn, reached forwards to throw on our down jackets.

Getting out of the plane and looking around, it was everything I wished it would be and more.

We were driven to Union Glacier and spent the night in a tent. The 24-hour sunlight was something we would apparently adapt to but, for now, we folded our buffs over our eyes. We woke to see six people clad in gloves and goggles lined up under a banner saying 'ANTARCTIC ICE MARATHON & 100K'. A gun went off and then they were gone, jogging off into the distance. Each to their own.

Another flight, this time in a Twin Otter plane, took us from Union Glacier to Vinson Base Camp and finally we could begin the expedition proper. Seeing this tiny plane take off in the pristine surroundings seemed extraordinary but, in Antarctica, it was the norm.

The format for the expedition would be similar to that of Denali, but with just one rope team instead of three. We split all our personal and team gear, tents, food and cooking equipment between a sled and our rucksacks. Every night we would erect our tents and the central mess tent would be dug into the ground.

Despite the potentially hazardous conditions in Antarctica, summit success rate was reasonably high on Vinson. As such, we could take it without much haste and truly appreciate the special environment we were in. The terrain for the first few days was not particularly demanding or steep so we just plodded on until we reached Low Camp.

Temperatures in the Ellsworth Mountains average around −30C with the wind chill regularly taking it down to −50C or so. Those sorts of figures seemed inconceivable before setting off, even after Denali and Everest, but with the right equipment, it appeared manageable.

The issue with the temperatures on Everest is the impact that the minimal oxygen has on one's body. At over 8,000m the body is struggling just to stay alive, even in benign temperatures. Your body struggles to keep the core organs warm and functioning; the thinning oxygen and thickening blood makes pumping it around, especially to the extremities, a greater consideration and fingertips and toes are almost sacrificed. On Vinson, the altitude was less extreme;

we fully wrapped up whenever we ventured outside, and this seemed to do the trick.

Henry David Thoreau once said, 'I love to be alone. I never found the companion that was so companionable as solitude.' One of my favourite times of day was at about 3 a.m. when I would rustle out of my sleeping bag, throw on a hat, jacket and gloves, make a cup of tea and just sit outside in silence. With a fresh chill in the air, it was refreshing and it would give me time to myself and the opportunity to be present in my own thoughts. It was my version of absolute tranquillity.

The small group allowed us to move quickly and efficiently. A hastily-thrown-together four-person team, in two tents for a number of weeks, can have its issues but, for the main, we worked cohesively. Robin, our team leader, was a knowledgeable alpine climber with plenty of Greenland experience. Pete, a retired molecular biologist, loved hill walking in Scotland and bell ringing, and George, a young guy still at school with Seven Summits aspirations, was in Antarctica as a Christmas present from his parents.

Again, it struck me that this can be one of the wonderful things about mountaineering expeditions. In spite of one's background, age, job or personality type, you have no choice but to work together. Socially the four of us would never have crossed paths; seemingly our only common interest was climbing. However, here we were, thrown together on an expedition to climb the highest peak in Antarctica.

Sir Ranulph Fiennes said when looking for teammates, 'We want people without malice, natural spitefulness or impatience. We want placid people who don't get too excited when things are going well or really down when they're going badly.' That is how, as a four, we had to be. Any disagreement or character difference had to be resolved as every meal, every climb and every night was to be spent in each other's pockets. It was testing at times. Learning to let things go, allowing for each person's quirks and embracing our setting became essential.

From Low Camp we made an acclimatisation run up the Headwall to cache food and equipment. The Headwall was the steepest part of the route and, on that move, we experienced a small insight into what Vinson could throw at us when conditions went from poor visibility to downright unpleasant as the winds picked up. We hastily moved to High Camp, erected our tent and huddled inside, complete with down jackets and gloves, and waited.

The weather refused to yield so we were left with no choice but to battle our way down to our food and equipment below. What began as a calm and relaxed day quickly morphed into a strong test of our resolve. We got back to Low Camp and for the ensuing few days were restricted to the confines of our tents.

Bing Crosby's 'Dreaming of a White Christmas' came to mind as we mustered the motivation to reinforce the snow walls of our tent on Christmas Day. Down suits, facemasks and heavy mitts were all required as we sawed away, cutting blocks of ice to form some semblance of protection against the elements. It was a total whiteout with raging winds and even inside our rattling tents there was a degree of tension and unease. We had no choice but to wait.

I opened Christmas cards from Klara and my family. This, as it always did, brought about emotional thoughts about what they were up to. It was another sacrifice. The faith they showed to stand aside and let me selfishly pursue this ambition was remarkable. It was a selfish ambition. I raised money for charity because, of course, I believed in the cause and I thought that what I was doing might raise some funds and awareness for something worthwhile, but this was something I wanted to achieve.

Klara never asked me to choose between the Seven Summits and her because I think she knew the answer and did not want to hear it. It was an all-encompassing obsession. I always apologised for the distress it caused to those close to me, but they knew it was something I felt I had to do and not making it my first priority would mean it would never come to a successful conclusion.

After a couple of days of hunkering down, the weather cleared enough to allow us out to stretch our legs and explore some of the surrounding area, including an ascent of Knutzen Peak. An enjoyable traverse along a rocky ridge helped us to rise above a low cloud line and gave us an unimpeded vision across this magnificent vista.

It was now time for the two-day push to the summit. Back up the Headwall we went and established our camp. Thankfully the tents were still intact after a bit of a battering, and we hoped the forecast would remain stable.

We arose to glorious sunshine and a clear day with the knowledge that somebody was looking down on us fondly. A few gently rising slopes led to a little incline where we overtook a Russian team and the summit appeared in full view ahead.

We felt fresh and like we needed to burn off some of the calories we had consumed while lounging in our tents for a couple of days. Instead of taking the normal route up, then, we took a steep route to the east which, while not technically demanding, was a nice lung-burner and allowed us to traverse the summit ridge. After a couple of hours, we approached the summit and were fortunate enough to be alone at the highest point in Antarctica.

The views were like nothing I had seen before. I had underestimated the size and scale of the Ellsworth Mountains but seeing the jagged peaks rise from the smooth landscape beyond was something very special. The temperature was agreeable, negating even the need for a down jacket. In no rush at all, the four of us took the opportunity to acknowledge what a truly remarkable place this was and one none of us was likely to visit again anytime soon.

My favourite ice cream shop in St Andrews, Jannettas Gelateria, have a challenge of how far you can take a Jannettas ice cream tub. I took a selfie with my tub and felt content that 10,000 miles from home in the most remote continent on earth was a reasonable effort. Owen, the owner, was chuffed when I showed him the picture and I have had ample supplies of their finest ever since. It was a worthwhile picture.

My video from the summit gave a good insight of how I felt at the time.

Video Diary – 28 December 2010

Yeah, we made it!! Great news. We are at the top of Vinson Massif, 4,892m, and it's pretty sweet up here.

For me, it's number five out of seven and the views are absolutely sublime.

There's a lot of vast open space, clear blue skies and we're down to just a jacket and a base layer. We've been incredibly fortunate. What a place!

We made reasonable time on our descent and moved to Low Camp in good spirits, before moving to Base Camp the following morning. The Russian team, led by Alex, the same man who hosted the soiree at Everest Base Camp earlier in the year, had beaten us down. I should have predicted what would happen, knowing the Russians I had come across...

'Ah, Geordie, you must be so thirsty. It is not so cold outside, nothing like Everest you agree. You have water?' he asked while handing over a bottle. I gratefully received it and, without thinking, took an enormous gulp. Alas, not water at all but vodka! Unsurprisingly, the Russians found it hilarious and we joyfully passed it round.

The Twin Otter took us back to Union Glacier and, after what seemed like a fleeting holiday visit, we were ready to depart. The final night in Antarctica was memorable. It was indicative of the rare spirit and camaraderie that exists amongst the fools who travel to weird and wonderful places around the world. After eating, we all relaxed in the knowledge that the weather was suitable for flying tomorrow. We were in a special location and what difference would a hangover make anyway?

With a range of nationalities and what appeared to be a limitless supply of the finest Russian vodka, the occasion had the ingredients for success. Every so often a different member of their team rose in his chair, warbled his favourite tune and shouted, '*Za zdorovye!*' a traditional drinking toast in Russia, translating as 'To your health'. We would all rise, toast and drink.

The Swedish contingent would follow up in due course with a hearty '*Skål!*' The Germans with '*Prost!*' and we Brits with 'Cheers!' And so the cycle would continue. The party went on well into the early hours and, finally, we all staggered back to our tents somewhat the worse for wear.

Leaving Antarctica was dispiriting. Not just because of the sore head but rather because it was like nowhere I had been before. Of all the places I have been fortunate enough to visit, the Antarctic landscape remains the most extraordinary. Even just visiting that continent was a privilege, but to stand at its highest point even more so.

In total contrast to the calming quiet of Antarctica, a hectic, stressful and haphazard few months lay in wait – and that was before the expeditions even began.

I had six weeks post-Vinson to sort out all the logistics and finances for back-to-back expeditions to Carstensz Pyramid and Everest in the spring. It was a fairly daunting prospect, but I had come so far that I did not really have a choice. I had to commit with everything I had to make it possible.

I needed new sponsors to be with me for the remaining two mountains and the completion of the Seven Summits project. Without them, it simply was not going to happen. As was the case before Vinson, I relentlessly pursued people and companies by phone and email utilising Thomas Edison's approach – 'I have not failed; I have just found

10,000 ways that won't work' – to motivate me. As before, even getting a negative response was pleasing compared with the silence that my approaches usually received. However, the genuine responses below brought about a sense of déjà vu.

> *We are running a very comprehensive marketing and sponsoring program in Europe and we are very committed to this plan.*
>
> *Unfortunately, we are not in position at this moment to expose ourselves to additional expense.*

Or

> *Thank you for your email. I have had a look over it and sent it on to our New Business Department. Unfortunately, this is not something we would be able to help you with.*

Things began to get desperate in mid-February. In a matter of weeks, I needed a significant amount of money to make any use of my flights from London to Jakarta. I called on all car dealerships and supermarkets nearby. I went to every local High Street bank I could, asked to see the manager, handed them my sponsorship pack and discussed the plan, but it did not go any further. I approached everyone from mountaineering brands and alcohol brands to watch companies and charitable funds.

Freddie and I made attempts to get musicians to do fundraising gigs for us but that fell flat on its face. On the plus side, it did lead to a couple of beers with Calvin Harris in the Green Room before he went on stage but not much further. Some of the more rash attempts to earn money rather than sponsorship included looking at medical testing, playing online roulette and applying for daytime quiz shows. Even an obligatory approach to Everest Windows got zero feedback. It was all in vain.

Despite the negative responses, I was also touched by the positivity that I received. For every email not replied to or message that happened not to be passed on to the right person, there was someone at the other end of the line who was willing to help and would think of others that could. Some of the people I contacted donated money to the RNLI because they admired what I was doing and thought it a worthwhile cause. It gave me cause for optimism. When the pressure continued to mount, I clung on to every ounce of hope I could rustle up.

Henry Wadsworth Longfellow said, 'Perseverance is a great element of success. If you only knock long enough and loud enough at the gate, you are sure to wake up somebody.'

I kept knocking and, thankfully, the University of St Andrews finally opened the door.

Geoff Morris from the university phoned me with good news. Geoff had been, since I had first met him a few months before, a huge believer in what I was trying to achieve, both for myself and for St Andrews. He persistently pushed through my sponsorship attempts, and his conviction that it would tie in nicely with celebrating the 600th year of the university finally came to fruition. They would sponsor my Everest 2011 attempt alongside Knight Frank Estate Agents. I was proud to receive the following endorsement from a place that meant a huge amount to me.

We often talk of 'scaling new heights' and 'climbing mountains', but few of us will ever have to face the challenges that Geordie Stewart has set himself. Geordie, whose passion for mountaineering developed at a young age, is hoping to become the youngest Briton to climb the highest mountain in every continent. I am delighted to offer my support to Geordie, who is a young man of great determination and resourcefulness. I hope that you will join me in wishing him every success in his forthcoming expedition.

Professor Louise Richardson – Principal and Vice-Chancellor: University of St Andrews

I had done my best with the search for sponsorship and got there in the end. It was an element of my Seven Summits attempt that went almost entirely unnoticed by the majority but it taught me as much as the climbs themselves. I did not have a silent backer or parent who could bankroll these expeditions as some youngsters do. Often I had wished I did, as it would certainly have made life easier. Equally, what a great learning curve to go through that process. It sometimes involved shameless and embarrassing moments, as well as constant rejection, but it taught me resourceful-ness and perseverance. I did not have those expeditions put on a plate for me but rather had to hustle my way to the start line and I am proud of having done it that way.

The weight off my mind after securing the funding to climb Carstensz and Everest was immense. Whether it be in professional sport or climbing mountains, all one can really try to do is control the controllables. It is easy to get distracted by things outside your control. In golf or cricket, for example, the best players are able to distance themselves from the scoreboard, from the heckling and from their past form. The best biathletes arrive at the shooting range and ignore the guy in the lane next to them and ignore the cheering fans. They focus only on what they can control.

I now had to focus on what I could control, which was to prepare the best I could physically and mentally for the two expeditions that lay ahead. Both would be challenging in different ways but, for the first time in a while, I was genuinely excited and hopeful about what was around the corner.

19

CARSTENSZ PYRAMID

4,884m / 16,024ft

Never say no to adventures. Always say yes, otherwise you'll live a very dull life.

Ian Fleming

Carstensz Pyramid would be the sixth mountain in my Seven Summits journey and it looked certain to be an adventure unlike anything I had done before.

I booked the climb with a local outfit to cut out the middle man and reduce costs. It made for a slightly questionable handover of a substantial amount of cash at Timika in Western Papua, but I was then good to go for the next few weeks.

I was bolted on to a team of seven suitably diverse and interesting Americans. We bonded instantly, which provided enthusiasm for the expedition. The first point of discussion was our kit list. It included wellies, waterproofs, an ice axe and an umbrella – not the usual requirements. This was not going to be a usual expedition.

There are two methods for approaching Carstensz – either by trekking to Base Camp, or getting a helicopter. The helicopter increases the cost and allows faster access. It also means avoiding controversies with local tribes, permits and the military. The British Foreign Office rates Papua in the 'travel at your own risk' category due to the Free Papua Movement fighting in the region. However, we had all opted for the extensive trekking route which, in itself, said a lot about the characters who had signed up.

Rumours of cannibalism in the region, political uncertainty, logistical difficulties and the dense jungle put people off Carstensz for many years. As such, there was disagreement in the climbing community about what constituted the Seven Summits. The American, Dick Bass, climbed Mount Kosciuszko in Australia in 1985 and, for some, that was deemed part of the challenge.

The great Reinhold Messner disagreed. He said the real Seven Summits involved Carstensz Pyramid, not Kosciuszko, based on the fact that the continent was inclusive of Indonesia not just the country of Australia. The first man to complete the challenge was Pat Morrow in 1986 who said, 'Being a climber first and a collector second, I felt strongly that Carstensz Pyramid, the highest mountain in Australasia... was a true mountaineer's objective.'

There are different ways of skinning a cat and when it comes to big mountains, people create their own parameters as to what they deem appropriate. It would be hypocritical to say I did every expedition in the purest manner. I used bottled oxygen on Everest and had a reasonable level of support, but my conscience was clear in terms of difficulty levels. For me the helicopter option was obviously an easier option, and choosing Kosciuszko over Carstensz was even more so.

We took a small plane and landed in Ilaga on a worryingly unsuitable runway. It made Lukla Airport in Nepal seem inviting, and that regularly ranks high on the 'World's Most Dangerous Airports' list. But we safely made it and were in a different world completely. All around was seemingly impenetrable jungle with thick mist billowing from the canopy. The contrast with the arrival in Antarctica could not have been more stark. We were greeted by curious specta- tors who looked highly confused by the alien visitors in funny clothing.

A trek to Suanggama, home to members of the Dani tribe, took us to where we would be staying for the next couple of nights. An evening of playing 'Hearts' and getting to know each other was a great way to start and, after a necessary sleep, we were intrigued as to what lay ahead.

We woke and were treated to a local Dani breakfast consisting of rice and sweet potatoes before being welcomed by the tribal leader. He appeared to give a rousing speech to the village but, in reality, could have said anything about us inappropriately located Westerners and we would have been none the wiser. Around us were enthusiastic and surprisingly talented children kicking a makeshift football and Dani tribesman grasping spears and wearing nothing but *kotekas*, or penis gourds.

To a person, we were clueless and awaiting direction. It transpired that quite a challenging 15km trek lay ahead. As a team, we concluded that any notion we had of itineraries or timetables had been thrown out the window somewhere on the airplane between Timika and Suanggama. We were just going to have to roll with the punches and keep an open mind.

Our team included Karl, a Californian banker whose daily working life was focused on key high finance deals, his NutriBullet and his exercise routine in the West Coast sunshine. Lilian was an eccentric New Yorker who lived in the apartment next to Quentin Tarantino. The pitch of her voice could pierce through the loudest of environments and yet her crazy squawk became something we all appreciated. Jim and David were family men from Colorado and Nevada respectively. They loved the outdoors, their children and seeing the world. Jim had also climbed five of the Seven Summits and would have Everest ambitions of his own in the coming years, if he could persuade his wife. David had spent a bit of time in London, had a cracking sense of humour and never failed to raise our morale.

We could see immediately why wellies were the footwear of choice. Those 15km predominantly followed the course of a river. Sometimes high above it, sometimes over it via a precarious bridge, and sometimes just straight through the thing. And then the river would veer off one way and we would go the other, only to be greeted by a knee-high, muddy swamp which we'd charge through due to lack of alternatives.

The brollies and waterproofs came out with the early afternoon storms. There are few things more irritating on an expedition than lugging items around that you never end up using, so to tick off so many within a few hours was a bonus. Upon reaching a version of a clearing, apparently Salt Factory Camp, albeit with a good bit of squelching underfoot, it was made clear to us that this was where we would be camping. We didn't have much choice in the matter, despite it appearing wholly unsuitable, so we set up camp and settled into more Papuan rice dishes.

The move from Salt Factory Camp to Indisaga will live long in the memory. Ascending about 1,000m and covering 17km seemed reasonable to our merry bunch, even after the sodden experiences the day before. We naïvely thought we were above the wetlands but oh, how wrong we were.

On went our wellies, with brollies and waterproofs at the ready, and we headed up a path from our riverbed camp. A few more bridges and river crossings emerged before we could make much progress. Plotting a route from one side to the other without a dramatic fall from grace into the water became the first key task. Once that was successfully navigated, we could move on and into the unknown.

The unknown transpired to be a beast of a day. It began by entering the rainforest and immediately ascending a fiendishly steep mud slope. Two steps up and one sliding back was the routine. It was a sign of things to come. For several hours we followed this mud trail through the dense jungle, enduring the insects and rainstorms as they came and went; over and under large roots and overhanging branches, through muddy swamps and across narrow fallen trees as large gorges loomed below.

Swinging on vines crossed our minds as a more efficient way of making progress through the heavy canopy, as our speed was negligible. A small clearing afforded us a rest stop to sit and wonder about what we had let ourselves in for. Todd and Eric were highly experienced guides, the former having summited Carstensz before with a client using the helicopter approach, but neither had seen anything like this – none of us had. One could climb for years in the Rockies, Alps or Himalayas and never experience this kind of nature. It immediately put into perspective our love for the clear crisp air of high snowy peaks, but, equally, we didn't want to be anywhere else. This was why we had chosen Carstensz over Kosciuszko and why we opted against the helicopter!

After our lunch break, we were straight back to it. We had mud splattered up our bodies and were soaking wet, but still, the rainforest would not relent. All altitude we appeared to gain up sharp waterlogged slopes would be lost sliding down the other side. Our porters, Dani tribesmen, appeared to have buggered off completely and were well out of sight. The last we saw of them was an old man with a weathered face and dark beard heading into the canopy, with a machete in one hand, wearing a luminous green hoodie. Written on his hoodie was 'Marijuana – The Magic Weed' with marijuana leaves printed all over it. Where he got it from I have no idea but it all added to the absurdity of the situation. They could have taken our bags anywhere and we would never have seen them again, so we kept our fingers crossed. Our initially high morale at the novelty was waning a little, but surely we must get to the end eventually.

Finally, and with great relief, we saw light ahead and our way out of the rainforest. We sat down and laughed at the ludicrousness of where we were.

'And to think...we paid for this!' said the consistently upbeat and witty David. The clearing afforded views of the terrain we had come across, treetops as far as the eye could see. Our joy was short-lived as the afternoon showers came crashing down, so on we went with barely a dry patch in sight.

I could not think why, but Indisaga reminded me somewhat of Salt Factory Camp. It probably had something to do with the softness underfoot, zero overhead protection and totally illogical location. We were tired enough that anything at that moment would do. It had been quite a testing day but, despite the dampness, we were grateful and somehow remained in good humour.

Mark Twain said, 'The human race has one really effective weapon, and that is laughter.' How true that is. Keeping a sense of humour when things get pretty shit can make all the difference – Ian's Borat mankini on Heather's birthday; Caesar's amusement at the 'Mate in a State' section from a crappy UK magazine on Aconcagua; the AK-47-clad border guards on Elbrus; the Russian team loading me up with vodka instead of water on Vinson. Humour is the human antidote to stress and fear. It temporarily alleviates concerns and brings a weary smile when nothing about a situation warrants it. Carstensz was the funniest expedition I have ever been on. It was tough at times but, through laughter, it also became one of my favourites.

Things were not that bad for us after the jungle day on Carstensz. We knew that nobody's life was in danger and that the Dani would not saunter off with our belongings. As such, we just embraced the comedy and thrill of where we were and who we were with. They are wonderful memories.

Having battled through that initial stretch, the terrain changed somewhat and, over the next three days, we would begin to make our way to Carstensz Base Camp at 4,273m. The altitude was not a huge concern for any of us. We had all been a lot higher and we had a gradual acclimatisation schedule.

We adapted to a new routine of wading through mud, battling the rain and marvelling at the Dani way of life. The topography morphed from the sharp inclines in the rainforest, to undulating boggy terrain amid shrubbery, into something like rolling Scottish moorland. We gained no more than 1,000m in three days; every day greeted us with novel problems, which required inventive solutions. They were long arduous days, but enjoyable.

Dr Wil Rose said, 'Success is not counted by how high you have climbed but by how many people you brought with you.' As a team we came to respect each other, were fond of the company we had and the times we shared together. Every day we would don the wellies, get out our walking sticks, and cover this boggy landscape, fascinated to see what lay around the next corner. We ambled and idly chatted in the late morning and midday sun. Our musical tastes aligned and as a group, with varying degrees of knowledge and singing ability, we would sing along to Bowie's 'Ziggy Stardust', 'Sympathy for the Devil' by The Rolling Stones and The Who's 'Pinball Wizard'. We could name a famous song from the 60s or 70s, my favourite periods of music, and off David would go reciting the lyrics. It was an enviable and useful skill.

When we felt like it, we would stop for a rest and bask in the tropical heat. We each improvised drying racks on the back of our rucksacks to allow for a regular change of tops, pants and socks, as they usually got drenched. And then the rain would settle in every day without fail around 2 p.m.. Back in the dry bags went our washing and out came the umbrellas. It rarely just drizzled – this rain was really committed to the cause. It was the sort of downpour that made us paranoid about whether our sleeping bags and warm kit were tightly sealed, as the rain hammered down on top of every conceivable bit of kit we possessed. We learned through trial and error what did and did not work, and just kept moving until the Dani told us to stop.

One thing we became fairly efficient at was river crossings and there were ample opportunities to refine our technique. Four options emerged really, depending on what sort of crossing it was. The first two involved staying dry (in theory), the latter two were the wet weather programme.

Option A: Find a narrow point and launch yourself across. Either wait for someone else to grab you at the far end or hope for a secure landing.

Option B: Go up and down the river to spot a suitable point for crossing using rocks in the water. This was a great test of route planning, stride length (a forte of Eric's) and balance.

Option C: Realise the futility in Options A and B, remove wellies, hurl them over to the far bank (not always successful resulting in a scamper downstream to recover a rogue boot), roll up trousers and wade through.

Option D: See the futility in Options A, B and C. Accept

one's fate and wade through regardless meaning wet socks and wet welly insides.

We came to the conclusion that options A (launching yourself) and C (welly hurl and wade) were the best courses of action. As I said: trial and error.

A significant element of this expedition was meeting the Dani. The tribe was unexpectedly discovered by the American philanthropist Richard Archbold during an expedition in 1938, and is one of the most isolated in the world. Beyond the *kotekas*, the penis gourds they wear, another distinctive part of their identity in contrast to the Western world is self-mutilation. After the passing of a loved one, relatives (nowadays just the women) are expected to cut off the top part of their fingers as a sign of respect and grieving. The practice symbolises the pain one feels after losing a loved one, with many people in the tribe amputating several fingers during their lifetime.

The Dani acted as porters during our expedition and their prowess and poise in the jungle was astounding. Their naturally wider feet – they were usually barefoot – allowed them to glide over thin branches that would leave us struggling for balance.

They were always kind and hospitable, as well as fascinated by some of our Western practices. They would watch with awe as we applied plasters to blistered feet and gesture they also wanted one. Happily, we would hand over a few and the next day some would be wearing them across their cheeks or arms as symbols of pride. When it came to sharing, I did have a limit. As one of them watched me brushing my teeth with total fascination one morning, he again insinuated that he wanted to give it a whirl. Without a spare in my bag, I had to say no, which left him peeved and confused.

Every night we would establish camp wherever they deemed suitable. On one occasion, as we sank into the mud on the far side of a river, they stopped, pointed downwards and signalled this was to be our spot for the night. After much deliberation and debate, they finally accepted our pleas and onwards we went to a more sheltered area. That was the only time; this was their home, we were the foreigners and we had to adapt to their customs, timings and wishes.

Every meal seemed to be rice-based; sometimes just rice. Thankfully, one of the team brought some sweet chilli sauce which, carefully rationed, just about made it through the trip and made the meals manageable. Sweet potatoes and bananas were the other staples – two things I'm fond of, not that we had a choice. The Dani gave us what they had, so our culinary options were somewhat limited to that and the snacks we had brought with us. Unsurprisingly, this frugal but functional diet was incredibly efficient for weight loss. Unlike in the past, this was far down on my priority list as Everest lay in wait a few weeks after my return from Papua.

When we set up camp, the Dani would hack up trees using their machetes and erect a large communal tent away from us. It was not customary to venture too near but sometimes I liked to watch and listen from outside. Smoke would billow through a vent at the top of the tepee from their earth oven – a method for cooking pig as well as their staples of sweet potato, banana and cassava. I could hear them gently singing in harmony and their peaceful, simple life made me think of the hectic nature of what we would return to in America and the UK.

The landscape began to change again as we gained altitude, neared the mountain and entered the heart of the Sudirman Range. Around us reared up other high peaks including Sumantri (4,870m) and Ngga Pulu (4,862m), a few metres lower in height than our objective. Gone was the vegetation of the wetlands below, gone was the rainforest, replaced by jagged, vertical rock faces lining the route.

We navigated our way up New Zealand Pass, technically a series of passes linked together, and scrambled through an interesting 50m-long climbing passage with a tough, slippery rock face. Instead of heavy rainfall at 2 p.m., we were greeted with driving snow, reminding us of the altitude gain. Another hour of this winding path took us to an empty Base Camp at the foot of an imposing rock frontage which was Carstensz.

We knew we would be heading for the summit at 2 a.m., which created a bit of excitement. We slept briefly before our alarms went off and we prepared our kit. Gone were the wellies and umbrella, replaced by karabiners, harness and helmet. An excellent day lay ahead.

We arrived at the base of the face in darkness, with our head torches illuminating the way ahead, and began our ascent. As is often the case with seemingly daunting rock climbs, when one gets up close, a suitable route emerges. Thankfully, the afternoon sunlight and lack of overnight rain had dried the rock and its sharp edges, although harsh on the hands, afforded excellent grip to enable our progress upwards.

We followed a series of gullies up the north face for about 600m of solid rock before breaking out onto the ridge. As the sun began to rise, our precarious position on the mountain became apparent. West we went, upwards along the ridge before coming across the main obstacle on summit day, known as the 'Gap'. We utilised a Tyrolean traverse – a method of using a fixed line to cross over free space or water – which meant attaching ourselves to the fixed rope and using a relay system to haul each other across this abyss. It took a bit of time to get everyone across but offered an opportunity to rest, eat and enjoy the process. Knee-deep snow covered the rocky summit ridge but the end was in sight and, not long after, we took our final steps to the peak of Carstensz Pyramid.

It was a great time of celebration in clear weather and we took photos and videos and savoured the moment. It was an excellent team, our morale was high and thankfully we could all celebrate together having made the top of this extraordinary mountain.

Descending added complications with the Tyrolean traverse Round Two but we all got through and made it back to Base Camp. Having successfully summited *Nemangkawi* – as the mountain is known in the Amungkal language – the next challenge was to get back to Ilaga. There did not appear to be a set timeline as to when we would move, how many days it would take, or when we were due to fly from Ilaga to Timika. We were, as we often said, on 'Dani Time'.

The Dani decided to make a move the following morning so we hurriedly loaded our rucksacks with plenty of snacks, not knowing quite how long we would be going for, and followed on. Down New Zealand Pass, and beyond our previous campsite, we were making good progress but did not want to jinx this forward momentum. As the rain came crashing down a bit later than normal, the Dani signalled where we were staying for the night and began the process of building their smoke den.

We had a feeling about what lay in store the next day. We were almost eager to hit the heavy rainforest again to see whether it was as arduous as our memories had us believe, and also to see the back of it. We headed that way in the morning and charged through the jungle as quickly as we could. After the ups and downs, the heavy mud and the 99 percent humidity, it was a passage we were glad to see the back of.

Getting back to Ilaga brought a sigh of relief and gave us, filthy and tired as we were, the chance to put our feet up under some sort of shelter. The tribal leader had again very kindly allowed us to use the other side of his hut for accommodation. We gratefully took the opportunity to lay out our Thermarests and get some well-deserved sleep.

A flight the following afternoon was convenient and hugely appreciated. Taking off from Ilaga runway was a tad more relaxing than landing, but, as we approached the edge of the cliff at the end, there was still an element of suspicion that we just might not make it. As the wheels parted from the runway, our distrust was released, and we bid farewell to the unforgettable rainforest below.

At Timika airport our team would separate, but not before gorging on plentiful quantities of steak and ice cream. Our weight loss had been fairly intense and, for once, wholly unappreciated. I headed to Jakarta and then back to the UK. Jim was off to Australia to work on his tan and the rest back home to the USA. It was a blow to leave them all but I'm immensely grateful to have shared those memories with such a humorous and resilient team.

My memories from Carstensz are unrivalled for their farcical and absurd nature. The expedition gave me enjoyable memories as well as hardship. The Dani, river crossings, the rain and an amazing rock climb on summit day made Carstensz and the trekking option the obvious choice – that sort of adventure is what life is all about. The uncertainty and constant bewilderment ensured it was a truly special experience.

Back in the UK in mid-March, I had two weeks to see Klara, my friends and family. But soon I would be saying goodbye again in preparation for what would – I hoped – bring an end to my Seven Summits mission: my second attempt on Mount Everest.

20

UNFINISHED BUSINESS

Give me six hours to chop down a tree and I will spend the first four sharpening the axe.

Abraham Lincoln

There is a saying that by 'failing to prepare, you are preparing to fail'. I made mistakes in how I prepared for Everest in 2010 and was keen to rectify those before I went back. I separated these into things I could do differently and things Adventure Peaks could do. I decided to climb with them again because of their guarantee to amend a few of the things that went wrong the previous year, something they acknowledged was not a success. They needed better communications during the expedition, more integrated use of Sherpas, staggered departure times and better food. Added to that, they offered a highly competitive price and, crucially, I could not see any better guiding company on the Chinese side of the mountain. There were 10 changes I needed to make in 2011:

1. *Training*. Take long multi-day trips to build specific endurance. Carstensz was perfect for this. The best way to train for climbing mountains is to climb mountains.

2. *Strength*. I lost an enormous of weight in 2010 and needed more muscle and fat reserves to burn off up the mountain.

3. *Timings*. Leave camps earlier, especially on summit day, to minimise the risk of exposure, darkness and personnel issues.

4. *Acclimatisation* 1. Acclimatising begins as soon as you arrive in Nepal. Ensure I maintain personal health prior to arriving at Base Camp.

5. *Acclimatisation* 2. Get up to 7,500m on the North Ridge on Phase Two of acclimatising.

6. *Wellbeing*. Remain healthy throughout and think long-term. Take vitamins and medication. Drink water relentlessly and keep throat in good condition.

7. *Food*. Find food I could eat at high camps. If it wasn't tasty at Base Camp, then it wouldn't be appealing above 8,000m. Get to High Camp early, stay hydrated and force myself to eat.

8. *Communications*. Take a radio. This was critical for safety and information for those back in the UK.

9. *Kit*. Bring disposable hand warmers to keep electronics and spare batteries warm on summit day.

10. *Attitude*. Enjoy it! You're climbing the highest mountain

in the world! I knew I *could* get there so I had to relax when I needed to, climb strong when it mattered and the summit would take care of itself.

Those two weeks went by far too fast. I went up to St Andrews to sort out sponsorship administration, as well as having a leaving dinner. My mates had adapted to this odd routine over the past few years but they supported me hugely, knew how much it meant and had faith I would get there.

Back in Hampshire I went to see Steve at his climbing shop again. I grabbed a banner of his to take up the mountain, not only because he promised me £500 for the RNLI but also to say thank you for his help. We discussed the battle plan for Round Two. I spoke with ex-teammates, fellow climbers and doctors about the trip. I had *Discovery Channel*, *Timeout* and other media commitments lined up as well as getting as much food in me as possible. Mum came up trumps on the latter, as I'd lost a significant amount of weight on Carstensz, due to the ropey rice diet. Lots of proteins and red meat to rebuild wasted muscle and lots of iron, in the form of spinach and liver, to build up my red blood cell count before we hit any altitude.

By the time the beginning of April came around, I felt prepared. I felt like the i's had been dotted and the t's crossed so now was the time to put it to the test. Last chance!

I think what worried my family and Klara, although they

never said it, was that they knew how much it meant to me. I think the decision I had made to turn around on my last attempt reassured them that I could think rationally up there. Equally, after getting so agonisingly close, they probably wondered how much I was willing to risk getting there this time around. We said our tearful goodbyes and I hoped the next time I saw them would be in celebratory mood in a few months' time.

The subsequent flight was a bit of a climbing reunion. Andy, Stephen, Mark and Heather had all been on the Everest 2010 team. The first three had made it high on the Northeast Ridge and, like me, wanted to finish the job. Heather had experienced terrible breathing issues at the North Col so she'd had to turn around and she had aspirations to get higher this time. We had all been in quite regular communication over the past six months but it was great to see them again.

Added to that, Jaysen, who had been with me on Denali a few years back, was also on the team – a strong climber as well as a thoroughly reliable and calm man, which made him a great addition – and Zac, our team leader. I had originally come across Zac on my first ever climbing course in Scotland all those years ago and here we were, about to tackle Everest. I enjoyed a sense of equilibrium. Overall, just having those people with me gave me immense hope and optimism for the challenges that were to follow.

We were delayed a few days in Kathmandu attempting to sort pre-climb administration. We were due to complete the same three-phase acclimatisation programme we had utilised in 2010. However, the Chinese authorities were not issuing permits for another few weeks so we had to use the time effectively to maximise our ability to cope with the move to Base Camp.

As such, we reverted to Plan B which actually turned out to be ideal as we would avoid staying in the unpleasant and dirty towns of Nyalam and Tingri, where we'd had to fight off vast swathes of rabid dogs with well-aimed walking sticks. Instead, we would fly to Lukla and make our way up the Nepal Everest Base Camp trekking route before returning to Kathmandu and driving to the Chinese Base Camp.

Flying to Lukla would have been terrifying a month before, but, after the Ilaga landing for Carstensz, I felt slightly more confident. The aim was to trek from Phakding (2,610m) near Lukla and end up touching 5,000m beyond Pheriche. It was planned to take around six days and would stand us in good stead when we headed back over to China.

While in Phakding I bumped into Dorje Khatri who would be one of our climbing Sherpas for the 2011 expedition. I had become very close to Dorje in 2010 and he had taken both my friend Jack in 2009 and then Matt in 2010 to the summit of Everest. 'Geordie, my friend!' he said, as his infectious smile and kind features came towards me. The first thing he declared was, 'This year, Geordie, we go to the top together. You and me. We reach the summit of Everest. I promise. OK?' I looked at his kindly face and said, 'Dorje, it would be the perfect end. I dream of that moment and, with you next to me, I don't have a choice but to make the top. I look forward to it, my friend.'

Trekking through the foothills of the Himalayas was something I had thought about for a long time, ever since reading Bear Grylls' book. Bear, like Edmund Hillary, had climbed from the Nepalese side. Seeing our itinerary include places such as Namche Bazaar, Tengboche and Pheriche conjured thoughts of the initial pull I'd felt towards Everest. The Nepalese side has an amazing history and part of me loved the idea of climbing famous features such as the Khumbu Icefall, the Western Cwm, the Lhotse Face and, of course, the Hillary Step. However, my heart was set on the Chinese side and, despite the statistics telling me otherwise, I had to trust my instincts.

We were not moving particularly fast and had time to gaze around at the gorgeous surroundings. It was heartening to observe the busyness of the route with yaks, Sherpas and trekkers all vying for space on narrow passes and even narrower bridges, with daunting drops into the valley below. We spent hours trekking past and camping opposite the iconic mountain Ama Dablam, seen as the 'Matterhorn of the Himalayas'. Nepalese prayer flags, used to bless the countryside, wafted in the gentle breeze and we diligently spun the prayer wheels to bring safety and hope in the challenges ahead.

The whole process was precisely what I'd hoped it would be. I felt extremely fortunate that our climbing permits had not been issued, allowing us to visit this side of the mountain. We got a glimpse of Lhotse and Everest for the first time and could see along the famous West Ridge. It seemed so unachievably far away and inaccessible given the terrain in between but many a climber had probably thought similar sentiments on the march to Base Camp.

It was, however, approaching peak climbing and trekking season and, despite initially being heartened, I found the numbers quite alarming. One of the joys of the north, despite its fairly austere conditions, is that there are no trekkers or tourists there. The Chinese deny them access. This means that the only people on or near the mountain are the ones attempting it, which reduces the queues and litter and thankfully keeps it more unspoiled. I enjoyed the trek through the Himalayan foothills but the sheer number of climbers and non-climbers on the south were a huge turnoff and I was comforted by my decision.

The majority of the team acclimatised well; more than half of us had been to over 8,000m, and it was an ideal introduction to the expedition. That first week was a suitably relaxed way to reconnect with my former teammates. Although we had spoken in fits and starts over the preceding nine months, hearing the 2010 summit-day stories of Mark, Andy and Stephen was enlightening. Despite the inquest after the expedition, there was still a lot of information that was new to me. Andy had had issues with his knees and equipment in the end but had managed to make it to the Northeast Ridge. Mark had turned around at the bottom of the Second Step and Stephen at the top of it. Mark and Stephen, in particular, had played roles in my own summit-day story.

I challenge anyone who makes a choice to turn around within a few hours of the summit of Everest not to have a slight tinge of *what if*. They all regretted the outcome. They lacked the contentment that some of our team had achieved, which is why they sought a return fixture to make amends.

21

EVEREST 2011

8,848m / 29,029ft

Mountains are both journey and destination...The summit, despite months of preparation and toil, is never guaranteed though tastes of sweet nectar when reached.

T.A Loeffler

We returned to Kathmandu, sorted administration and then made the move to Everest Base Camp. There was a sense of déjà vu in our vehicle as we swung around blind corners at breakneck speeds, helplessly eyeballing the abyss below. It would be a shame to have such aspirational Everest summiteers all perish in a tragic road accident en route to the mountain, but it was out of our hands. We did, mercifully, make it across Friendship Bridge into China and headed out on the calm asphalt across the Tibetan Plateau.

Tingri seemed different when we drove through. In the nine months since our last visit, someone or something had taken action. The rabid dogs were not totally absent but dramatically lower in numbers. I thought that even George Mallory, so disparaging of the place, would be looking down with a wry smile.

And then there it was, in all its majestic glory once again: Mount Everest! It appeared as foreboding as I remembered, looking down on us from high and challenging us to make the first move. As Jaysen said, 'The first visions of Everest are very thrilling. Then I remembered we were actually going up there and it turned into quite a scary prospect.' Upon arriving, I immediately lugged my bags over to the furthest tent and again gave myself a gorgeous uninterrupted view of it.

The character of a mountain does not change. Over time some of its features might alter or its conditions might differ year on year, but its character stays constant. Everest is a big, uncompromising, unforgiving beauty of a mountain. Climbers may reach the summit without significant drama, they may even experience calm weather and zero avalanches, but the mountain will always have the final say. Everest will be the one that decides who gets the chance to make the summit and who does not. We aspiring fools do the best we can; we control our controllables. At the end of an expedition, whether one is even given the opportunity to try for the summit or not is down to the mountain.

Irritatingly, I had picked up a bout of food poisoning in Kathmandu. It was most likely from ice cream, which is not a wise choice in a country like Nepal with its questionable water supply. For four days I was on a diet of Pringles and flat Coke. Everything else I attempted to eat, much to my angst, did not enjoy residing in my stomach and sought the quickest possible exit. I felt weak at 5,200m and the altitude hardly did much to arrest my fears. As with Matt in 2010, I would be at high risk of HAPE and a potential evacuation. Thankfully, it cleared, my morale increased and we were good to go.

In contrast to the depressive period I suffered in the summer of 2010, my perspective on the mountain was different now. Again, as Lao Tzu said, 'If you are depressed, you are living in the past. If you are anxious, you are living in the future. If you are at peace, you are living in the present.' I had moved away from the past. I still thought about it, of course, but not in the same brutally self-critical way. Equally, I was certainly not at peace yet; I was anxious. I was thinking about the future. I wanted to fast forward six weeks, get to summit day, get to 8,700m and crack on past the point where I had turned around. I felt almost indignant that I had to spend so long retracing my steps just to complete such a small stretch of land. That is the nature of mountain climbing and I was going to have to get on with it if I wanted to get to the top of Mount Everest.

Mountain climbing is fundamentally illogical. Such struggle, hardship and risk and for what? Fifteen minutes on top with a pleasant summit picture and view if the weather is kind. That's the physical reality, for some, but I say it flippantly because it is not how I see it. Mountains do more than that. They liberate the soul and they free the mind from the chaos of life. They allow the imagination to escape and enable the body the chance to express itself in the natural world. Mountains are so simple and yet running through them is a complex and beautiful tapestry, woven together to allow humans to test the core of their spirit to its limits.

Video Diary – 13 April 2011

My eyes seem permanently fixated upon a little area, high on the Northeast Ridge, just below the Third Step and 150m from the summit, where I turned around in 2010. I imagine that will be a common theme this year until I, hopefully, get the chance to stand at its highest point.

I was totally focused on one point on the Northeast Ridge. I knew I could get there. I knew the route to that point, felt comfortable with the logistics, felt content with the altitude. But what about that final 150m? I had been told by many people it is just a quick scramble up the Third Step, hit the summit slopes and you are pretty much there. Except I had not experienced that. I had experienced pretty much everything on 23 May 2010, including hypoxic climbers, intense fear, dwindling oxygen supplies and crevasses, but I had not experienced that final 150m and I had not experienced the summit.

———

Within a few days at Base Camp my oxygen saturation levels had normalised and I was back in. One of the first things I did was return to the Everest memorial at Base Camp. I paid my respects to George Mallory and Andrew Irvine, but I was really focused on a new memorial that had emerged since I was last on the mountain.

PETER KINLOCH
SUMMITED MAY 25 – DIED MAY 26 2010

Peter died on the final climbing day of the 2010 Everest season. He summited late, at 1 p.m., but shortly after his summit, he was struck by snow blindness. He began to stumble and lose coordination. It took him almost four hours to get from the summit to the base of the Second Step – a section that should take one. Three Sherpas struggled for almost eight hours to bring Peter down, bringing him drugs, food, water and oxygen. At 5.30 p.m., as darkness fell, they were forced to abandon him when frostbite and hypothermia began to set in.

Peter, aged only 28, was left to die alone on the Northeast Ridge.

I knew Peter and we had spent time together at Base Camp and higher up in 2010. His team went for the summit a few days after us. He was an IT specialist and an Inverness Caledonian Thistle football fan – we bonded over Scotland and football. I was 21 but 28 was still so young and he had such life ahead. I thought to myself:

How did you manage to run out of oxygen?
Why didn't you just turn around earlier, Peter?
Why did you summit so late in the day at 1 p.m.? Our turnaround time was 11 a.m.. We had the same choice to make.
Was it worth it? To achieve your dream but cut short your life in the process.

Those of us who had been here in 2010 quickly settled into the old routine. We drank water, played Risk and idly sat around getting to know our new teammates. Added to that, we got in some good acclimatisation treks up to 6,000m, which stood us in good stead for Phase One of the expedition – reaching the North Col.

We had our *Puja*, blessing us and the mountain. We hoped it would be more successful than the previous time. The prayer flags went up all around Base Camp and this barren landscape suddenly became a sea of colours and hub of activity. Each team had their own little section of Base Camp, the same as last year. The Russians had the advantage of being nearer the mountain and out of the wind. We, like the Aussie team, were slightly exposed but nearer the satellite hotspot and trekking route. Amazingly the Swiss got it worst of all by being unprotected from the wind, furthest from the mountain as well as furthest from the satellites. A rare lack of efficiency was not missed by anyone and they didn't like to be reminded of it.

We moved to Advanced Base Camp (ABC) after splitting the 16-mile route into two days and rested there a few days before moving up the Headwall. The team seemed in reasonably good shape. We had 15 climbers and the reduced numbers seemed to be highly beneficial for efficiency and logistics.

The other team leader for the expedition was Chris, a super laidback Canadian climber. He was highly experienced with multiple K2 attempts as well as Cho Oyu and Broad Peak summits. He seemed to spend his life moving from one expedition to another, and would provide valued technical advice plus an enviably nonchalant approach.

The rest of the team comprised a range of ages and life experience. Ben's 'Adventure CV' stood out immediately: a no-nonsense Yorkshireman from Leeds, he had been an amateur footballer before setting about his 'to do' list, and now regularly competed in ultramarathons including the Marathon des Sables – six marathons in a week in the Sahara – and 100-mile races. He had achieved unsupported Atlantic rows and the fastest British crossing of Greenland. It seemed total masochism but was impressive nonetheless.

Greg was a lean, athletic and good-looking Welshman who worked in London. He was coy about some of his achievements but they began to reveal themselves as the monotonous days wore on during the trip. He worked in finance predominantly but had a string of 'other ventures on the side' as well as being a keen surfer and techie. In different ways, I got on well with both Ben and Greg from the start. I appreciated their approaches to life and what they had achieved. Along with the returning climbers and Jaysen, I felt buoyed about our chances. The major test was to come.

I had been up the Headwall to the North Col three times by now, so felt fairly relaxed about what to expect. In contrast to the trepidation of the year before, I was genuinely excited to get on the ropes and gauge my level of fitness and strength.

'Pretty shite weather,' I said to Jaysen as we set off. 'But we should get up there in three or four hours, have a bite to eat and head back down again.'

He later said, 'That was up in the list of top toughest days of my life – I was suffering a lot.' The first time I did it in 2010 had stirred similar emotions, as I wondered how the hell I was ever going to get up to the top when I could barely drag one foot in front of the other at 7,000m. This time was great, however, and I made it up in about two and a half hours, feeling quite comfortable throughout.

The weather was pretty nippy at the Col and I was clad in goggles and mitts to keep warm while getting food on board. I probably pushed it a bit but not that much. I wanted to see where I was at and reassure myself about how I was coping at altitude. The route meandered around the large serac that had killed the Hungarian climbers in 2010; the snow colouring and some of the debris were still evident on the route twelve months on. It was also odd to think that, the last time I was here, I'd been in a truly dire state and Matt had battled his way out of a crevasse having gone in up to his armpits. What a difference a year makes.

It turned out that extended periods of trekking through mud, rain and jungle had been quite good training after all, so I could tick the box I wanted, chill at the North Col and then head back to Base Camp. It felt, all in all, a successful venture and Phase One was complete. The communications below give an indication of where my head was at and what I was thinking about.

Email to family – 29 April 2011

Hope you are all well. I am feeling very happy and content at

Base Camp. 4hr descent from ABC yesterday was fine, bit of a bore – number four out of six – but nice to be back.

What else is new? Phase One is complete and I feel in good shape. I have about 100 Strepsils so am trying to take care of my throat as much as possible.

Physically, I feel very good. The difference between last year and this is almost incomparable so I just hope I can keep that up. One big push to 7,500m on Phase Two then summit bid for Phase Three :)

Fingers crossed for the weather.

Miss you all. Lots of love. G xx

The majority of the team fared reasonably well on their push to 7,000m. For quite a few it was a new altitude personal best, having reached the summits of Aconcagua and Ama Dablam beforehand. After what had happened in 2010 I knew that, like it or not, the members of our team *might* be the ones relied upon to save someone's life further up the mountain.

We rested for a few days before heading back up the mountain. As a result of the delays in Kathmandu and our forced acclimatisation trek in Nepal, we were a little bit short of time and thus a week behind our 2010 itinerary. This in itself was not a massive drama, but it had the potential to be, if our only weather window was earlier than expected. It meant I had to ensure I made good time on Phases One and Two and then rest sufficiently to give me the best possible chance come our summit push.

22

FOREVER UPWARD

If you cannot understand that there is something in man which responds to the challenge of this mountain and goes out to meet it, that the struggle is the struggle of life itself upward and forever upward, then you won't see why we go.

George Mallory

'Climbing high but still sleeping pretty damn high' was our approach for Phase Two in the acclimatisation process. As Greg said, 'Part of Everest is trying to understand your own body. If you go to Base Camp and climb to the summit, it takes five days. But the reality is that Everest doesn't take five days, it takes two and a half months because you need to acclimatise, you need to go up, you need to go down.'

As we made our way back to ABC and back up the Headwall, I no longer had concerns about adaptation to altitude, fitness levels or the route ahead. Instead, I was calm and enjoyed where we were, while remaining zeroed in on what I wanted to achieve along the way. I had structured in my mind the key boxes to tick during my time on the mountain. Getting one's head around the objective was important for my mental fortitude. Gone was the fear of '*Can I do this?*' and in its place was '*Let's do this, you know you can.*'

I have friends who compete at a high level of sport and fellow mountaineers who don't have that first-time fear. Those athletes and mountaineers have an unwavering belief in their own ability. Perhaps it is a hangover of mine from my teenage years, but I have to prove it to myself by having done it, while they have it from the off. They can enter a contest and back themselves, their bodies and their minds to beat off the competition and succeed. It is enviable in many ways, not having that self-doubt or fear of failure.

Greg was probably in that category. He was systematic and organised in how he went about the climb in terms of nutrition and timings, but he also possessed a lot of self-belief. He had done the research and spoken to enough people that he believed in himself and his chances of success. Greg, Jaysen and Ben were strong during the first few phases of the expedition and I looked forward to reaching the higher slopes with them. Andy and Stephen also seemed to be in good shape for their second attempt. Perhaps the fear of what was ahead had been overcome by them too. Either way, I felt pretty confident that, come our summit bid, those five would be alongside me.

My tentmate at the North Col felt pretty ill at that altitude so headed down, leaving me on my tod which was pleasant, if a little chilly. The body heat and breathing of a tentmate has a huge impact on the temperature within, but it was nothing that bad, so I prepared my food, listened to some Van Morrison, and got a bit of shuteye before starting early the next morning.

Blog – 5 May 2011

I woke at 5.30 a.m. on 5 May, my 22nd birthday, to a condensation-ridden, sodden, tent but to clear blue skies. After a couple of hours of boiling water and hydrating, it was onto the North Ridge.

500m of unrelenting ascent up a snow line where the terrain rarely changes and one's mental fortitude is tested constantly.

It was draining. The slope just never seemed to end and each false crest brought with it a groan from within. Finally, the snow slope yielded. Out of a team of fifteen people, including two leaders, only five of us made it to the checkpoint of 7,500m. In itself that doesn't mean much but psychologically it was a great point to reach and the view was wonderful.

It was a hell of a birthday and one I certainly won't forget. The lonely wake-up-and-shiver was certainly a shock but the extra admin space was a bonus. I could chaotically throw my things around the tent rather than carefully splitting it 50-50 and attempting not to encroach on someone else's personal space. At 8 a.m. we all clambered out, gave each other a smile and headed up. I went with Andy the whole way; I think we had an unspoken synergy in how we wanted to approach the mountain this time around.

The progress was slow, monotonous and challenging. Sometimes you are at the base of a big climb or the beginning of a race and are just not feeling it. You are there on the start line but you know something is not quite right. Something is amiss in your body or mind that is saying, 'Today is going to be really tough and I'm not willing to suffer. Or indeed, I am willing to suffer, but it's going to be extremely unpleasant.' On other days, like my birthday, you wake and are enthused about the suffering. You know it's going to be hard, you know it's going to hurt and your body will be strained but that's alright. It's alright because you also know that you're going to get the job done.

Andy, Ben and I took some pictures and headed down. We knew that we had ticked a really important psychological box. The difference between getting to 7,300m and 7,500m is negligible in reality, but it was a target we had set ourselves and completed. Heading down that snow slope again brought me back to 2010 with Matt and Pete when, exhausted, we had battled to locate our tents and force our legs to move in a vile storm. However, I smiled as I trundled down and thought about how we eventually made headway in our three-man bobsled. I laughed at the mental image of us, exhausted and helpless in our yellow down suits, doing our best to re-enact *Cool Runnings* in a total whiteout. I knew those guys would be following my progress; I had spoken with them before heading out, and I hoped finally to be able to celebrate with them properly, all having achieved the same dream.

Fingers crossed it was the penultimate time I would make my way down the East Rongbuk Glacier. I kept myself motivated by going quicker than before, listening to upbeat music and dreaming of doing it only once more, when I would be gleeful after having just summited. We made it down to Base Camp and Dorje was there with a Nepalese silk scarf, and the words, 'Happy Birthday, Geordie. Best, Dorje Khatri', written on it. It would be a treasured possession from that moment on.

23

PATIENCE

A man watches his pear tree day after day, impatient for the ripening of the fruit. Let him attempt to force the process, and he may spoil both fruit and tree. But let him patiently wait, and the ripe pear at length falls into his lap.

Abraham Lincoln

It was just a waiting game. We got down to Base Camp on 8 May and then we could do nothing more than patiently wait for the weather window to emerge, and remain as healthy as we could for when it did. *Chomolungma* had to open her doors to us and until that moment we had to remain.

For 10 days, without exception, there were summits from Nepal; a steady flow of people heading into the Death Zone and standing on the summit. That gave me hope but it also brought frustration within the team as we remained stranded. *Would we even get a chance?* The weather in the south was consistently better year on year – part of the reason people opted for that side – and this year was no different.

Dorje came running to my tent one morning, starting shaking it and said, 'Geordie, Geordie, come outside. You enjoy this, I promise. I sorry if I wake you but you must see.'

I clambered outside and whirling around the summit of Everest was a red parachute. It floated aimlessly in the winds and then disappeared from view – astonishing. One of the Nepalese Sherpas, Babu Sunuwar, from the south had parachuted off the summit. It was a hell of a thing to see and how it must have felt, I can only imagine. I thought of the ease of that descent – assuming a safe landing, of course. Apparently, he made it down in about 18 minutes, compared with our three days and multiple nights.

So on we waited, day after day, getting more news of summits from the south and hoping the conditions would turn in our favour. Then another issue emerged: that of rope fixing.

Much of the route to the summit had fixed ropes with snow pickets driven into the ground to secure them. On the south, the climbing teams share the workload and cost associated with it. This is always a cause for controversy, as solo climbers and small teams receive all the benefits but do not share the cost. In China, however, the ropes were being fixed by the Chinese Mountaineering Association (CMA) and nobody was allowed to proceed up to the higher camps until they did. The earliest it would be done was 18 May, but even that seemed ambitious.

A number of teams moved to ABC in preparation for a summit attempt thanks to a weather window, only to be told by the CMA they could not go up. As the body does not recover at 6,400m as it does at Base Camp, we were in a stronger position than those teams who rolled their dice without success.

> Email to family – 14 May 2011
>
> *There are some pissed-off teams at ABC who have a dilemma – either wait at ABC or come back down to Base Camp. It has certainly caused a bit of controversy on the mountain.*
>
> *Loads of summits on the south right now. Bastards got their ropes fixed ages ago and have good weather. Different ball game over here.*
>
> *The jet stream appears to be hitting the mountain around 19–21 May. After that, the winds should drop which is when we hope to go – maybe 23–26 May.*
>
> *Not much else to say. Miss you all lots. xx*

A consideration in the delay at Base Camp, as in 2010, was one of acclimatisation. In the same way the body builds red blood cells to allow it to go high, it also rapidly loses that benefit, usually after a couple of weeks. I spoke to Jake back in the UK about his experiences and the potential need to re-acclimatise if the situation arose that we would be stuck for more than a few weeks.

We listened to music, read, went for walks and played cards. Patience is a virtue and we just had to wait. There was no other option. '*If you can wait, and not be tired by waiting...*'

Kipling's words ran through my head day after day as each negative forecast came through and I just hoped we would get our chance.

On a daily basis, I would look at photos of my family, of Klara, and of my friends dotted around the tent. Their love and support was so key to me, and without knowing it, they gave me strength at this time. I read letters and messages that people had given me before I headed out and would use their kindness and wisdom as extra motivation.

> *I'm sure you'll have an exhilarating time mate. You know most of the route anyway so should be fairly simple. Seriously though best of luck and wishing you all the success and safety in the world. I look forward to following your progress...while sat here in my armchair with the heating on!*

> *I honestly thought you were going to come back with another summit under your belt when you set off a year ago. As you depart now for your second attempt, I wish you my absolute best.*

> *Onwards, and in your case, upwards. We will be thinking of you every step of the way.*

> *While the pressure on this trip, more so than before, may be high, I trust that you will exhibit the same level of wisdom that you always do on the hill...be a wise mountaineer my friend.*

And then the good news came. Zac came down from getting his daily forecast and a window seemed to emerge. The temperatures were rising and, more importantly, the winds were dropping. He made a decision that we would move the following morning, 21 May. The hope would be to summit on 26 May after a move to ABC, a rest day, and then bouncing consecutively from the North Col to Camp 2 and then to High Camp and the summit. A tough schedule but this was what we had waited for.

That information set in place a frenzy of activity within the team, as people made last-minute preparations and sent final emails to loved ones.

It was also, like last year, a good chance to chat to the team about their motivations and desires for higher up the mountain. There were similarities but with subtle differences. Some wanted the ego boost and the story to tell, others had a childhood dream they wanted fulfilling while some just wanted to see if they could do it – to see if they could climb Mount Everest. Either way, we all had made a decision to climb the mountain, had followed through with that aim and now were about to embark on a gruelling week-long journey that might just take us there.

With the focus now on getting up the mountain, we could move to ABC and the North Col with a sense of relief and excitement. This was it. There was a final chance for me to email my family, Klara and Freddie about what was to come.

Email to family – 20 May 2011

Weather forecast is good. I am leaving Base Camp tomorrow and should summit on 26 May. Fingers crossed. Such a relief this is happening. We have a window. A couple of logistical things:

a) Because the ropes are now fixed, every other team should have gone through meaning the route will be established and it'll just be us up there which is ideal.

b) Summit day itself. We had a long meeting about this yesterday and the logistics are now smoothed out. We have staggered departure times, oxygen bottle checks, radio checkpoints (everyone has one) and appropriate communications to the UK.

I just want to say a huge thanks to each of you. None of you has ever questioned, at least not to me, that I wouldn't succeed in this Seven Summits project and have shown nothing but support from the very first time I mentioned it.

Your support has been invaluable, I couldn't have got here without it and I am massively grateful for that.

I love you all. I will stay safe and promise I will make the most prudent decisions when it comes down to it. I can't wait to speak to you all after our summit attempt, only then it will be a success.

Lots of love

Geordie

24

THE TIME IS NOW

The secret of success in life is for a man to be ready for his opportunity when it comes.

Benjamin Disraeli

There was some apprehension about what was ahead. Most of us had made it up the North Ridge within a few hundred metres of each other before, and were aware of the pain we were about to put ourselves through.

I was planning not to use oxygen until Camp 2 at 7,800m. I knew I could get to 7,500m, so if I could hold out just a little bit further, I decided, I would then get a big boost when I needed it most. This went against everything I believed in terms of maximising strength in preparation for summit day, but I had got it in my head that it was the *right way to climb Everest*. Utter shite really – whether you take it at

7,000m or higher, you're still on bottled oxygen, so why not put the odds in your favour? I would regret the decision immensely.

I had had some tough battles on the North Ridge 12 months previously, from blistering heat and vicious crosswinds to total whiteouts and deep snow – but the move to Camp 2 on 24 May takes the biscuit.

I started the day with a freeze-dried meal of porridge and raisins. My initial progress was good as I diligently made my way up, but then it all started to go pear-shaped. I had been at the front the entire expedition and felt really strong, but when all of a sudden everyone else in the team charged past me with their oxygen masks on, it affected me psychologically. They were sustaining a pace I could not match and the negative emotion of regret began to enter my mind.

I was lost in my own thoughts and self-loathing all the way up that bloody slope. *You idiot, Geordie. Why didn't you just take oxygen? You stubborn prick. You don't need to prove anything. FUCK! Nobody will care whether you used oxygen or not but you've just screwed up your whole summit attempt. Four years and you've fucked it with one stupid decision. Idiot!* I was struggling to keep going.

A few hours lost in my own head and the frustration of struggling behind the others was enough to totally change my perspective. The pain in my back I had previously suppressed had come to the surface. I was throwing up the meal I had in the morning and my mind was collapsing – it wanted to give up, it wanted to give in. *Maybe this is too much for me, maybe Everest is just too much for me.* I thought of the letter I had received saying, 'Be a wise mountaineer, my friend.' *Maybe this is what he meant. Knowing when to quit, knowing when enough is enough and turning around.*

Video Diary – 24 May 2011

This is very very hard work, and very slow moving. It's been a bitch of a day so far, to be honest. I'm constantly filled with the regret that I should have taken oxygen lower down. I've just been sick which is not ideal. Maybe in a few hours, I get to 7,500m and get some oxygen. This is a tough tough day. Fuck I hope I get there.

Something in the deep recess of my mind told me to keep going, that this pain would not last forever, that I just had to get to 7,500m. I needed to search for *sisu* once again. I needed an extra gear, a psychological boost – something, anything. *Sisu* is about enduring in the face of adversity. It is about finding the courage within to refuse obstinately to yield. I needed to find *sisu*, or it was over.

Two days, Geordie, just two days until the summit. Just get through this. Keep going. Think of all the training. Think of all the people back at home who have supported you. Think of the pain and anguish you went through last year. Two fingers to the people who thought it was impossible. Two fingers to the people that said you couldn't do it. Don't screw it up now, mate. Keep going. Do not stop. Do not give in. You cannot give in!

Jacob was alongside me now. I appreciated the company but he was in a deep world of hurt as well. I finally dragged myself up to the top of the snow slope, put on my oxygen mask and a deep relief came over me. Perhaps it was psychological, perhaps it was the genuine impact of the oxygen. Regardless, I felt exponentially better and knew I would make it to Camp 2. The last time I made it to 7,500m, without oxygen, it had taken me six hours. On this day it was more like nine and we still had a few to go. It was one of the hardest days I could remember and I didn't really understand why.

Darkness came and I finally collapsed into a tent with Stephen who had kindly prepared food and water for me. He had heard me on the radio and knew I was in a bad way. His teamwork made a massive difference that day. I took off my gear and relief swept over me. Relief that I had made it through a pretty hellish 12-hour day and relief that *sisu* had kept me going – that I did not yield. There are always times on expeditions when you have to dig deep, however experienced you are, and, after a relatively unruffled trip for me so far, I really had to graft to get there. I had proved to myself and my fragile mind that I was willing to suffer.

Because of the effects of altitude, it can become one of the most torturous exercises to actually eat anything. You've burned so many thousands of calories, so you should be starving and happy to eat anything in front of you, but that's not how it works. My body struggled with the freeze-dried meal, so instead I opted for as many Pringles as I could eat. Pringles aren't my favourite food by any means, but in that environment I knew I could stomach them, and they would give me the calories, salt and fat my body so desperately craved. With an expected 30,000 calories to be burned over the next few days, it was about trying to make up the deficit as much as possible. A scratch on the surface perhaps but a scratch nonetheless.

Despite the misery of the previous day, I somehow woke with utter focus and determination. I wanted to set off at a reasonable time and make good speed to High Camp but I had no idea how my body would feel.

Thankfully, my body clearly felt the same. Without it seeming as though I was working particularly hard or stretching my capability, I began to move past the rest of the team and was happily out in front. It was baffling to me after the move to Camp 2 but I was not going to complain. Somebody said to me that these expeditions are like playing poker: 'You have to minimise your losses and maximise your gains.' The day before was about minimising my losses but this was about maximising gains, getting to High Camp in good time and preparing for my summit bid.

Dorje saw me up ahead and a few hours from camp he caught up and we moved together. 'You very strong today, Geordie. This is good. Better than yesterday! You were not so strong then. You must be tired but I happy you here. Tomorrow,' he said, pointing upwards, 'we go there together. Like I promised, you and me. Leave at nine and we make the summit.'

'Yes, Dorje. Damn right. We'll get there together!'

The view was spectacular as these zagged Nepalese mountains started to appear below our eyeline. The sun was beating down and, despite being in the Death Zone, a major struggle was coping with the heat and avoiding dehydration. I had my down jacket and salopettes unzipped to allow the wind to cool my body but it made for tough conditions.

Not everyone on the team was going to be able to make the summit and some people had to make the tough decision to turn around. Unfortunately, Heather barely made it past 7,200m due to breathing issues, so she returned to ABC – it was her second attempt and once again she had tried hard but it was not to be. Simon also decided to call it a day halfway up the North Ridge. He was resilient but, in his words, 'What is more important, reaching the top of a mountain or seeing your new grandson?' I respected his decision. He returned to ABC to coordinate all the communications from there – an essential and undervalued role. Jacob, who had accompanied me up the snow slopes on the North Ridge, did not get past Camp 2 due to severe kidney problems; he was a valued teammate so it was a shame he had to turn around. Nick made it to High Camp, but no further. Making that sort of altitude is a superb achievement and, like Ian in 2010, you know when you're at your limit.

Slowly the compassionless mountain was winning the battle against the fragility of humans.

I made it around 1 p.m. and immediately set to work for my 9 p.m. departure with Dorje. An important part of what I wanted to do differently was to arrive at High Camp in far better condition than I did in 2010. Then, I arrived as it was getting dark after gruelling back-to-back days and was looked after by Matt and Pete before a quick turnaround for our summit bid – something I was dreading. This was different as I felt in good shape, albeit pretty tired, and was now focused on doing what I could do to maximise my chances.

Video Diary – 25 May 2011

I've got to High Camp at 8,300m. It's the highest camp in the world. I've just spent the last 20 minutes to get ice and snow to boil. Hydration is so important. I'm pretty tired, I need to rest for the next six or seven hours and get food in me.

At the moment the winds are pretty calm. There was a bit of a snowstorm earlier but that seems to have disappeared. You never know what can happen but I'll give it my best shot.

I spent the next seven hours over the stove in a tent with Ben. He'd made decent time but was certainly having a battle. When I asked him how he felt on video, a slightly puffy and weary man huddled in his down suit turned to me and said, 'I feel like I could go to sleep.'

25

SUMMIT DAY – 26 MAY 2011

Our greatest weakness lies in giving up. The most certain way to succeed is always to try just one more time.

Thomas Edison

At 8.45 p.m., I unzipped the tent and felt a gentle breeze in the night sky. On went the harness, crampons and three 3.5kg O2 bottles strapped to my rucksack. At 9 p.m., I was ready to go. Mentally I was in the right place. I felt prepared. I knew where everything was: my spare mitts, hand warmers, spare head torch, spare camera, summit flags, emergency meds. Physically I felt strong. I was going to summit Everest! But there was no sign of Dorje.

Come 9.15 p.m., I was frustrated with waiting, so set off alone in the dark, sure that Dorje would catch me up. I found those first few hours absolutely exhilarating. There was fresh snow, so I was breaking trail alone on Mount Everest. It was a privilege to be absorbed by the imposing silence of the mountain.

Video Diary – 25 May 2011 10 p.m.

This is what life is all about. 10 o'clock at night, breaking trail, fresh snow and not a head torch in front of me. This is bloody brilliant. Awesome place to be. Absolutely awesome.

Dorje caught up as I hit the Northeast Ridge. He just followed my footsteps, knowing that we were making good time. It was tiring work certainly, the soft snow often meant we would slip back after every few steps. At 8,500m it was tough but we alternated leading to keep us both fresh. Our weary bodies clambered over rock steps and through gullies. It was exciting leading the pack with no other head torches to illuminate the route ahead. After the First Step – a 10m rock scramble – our progress was halted by a couple of things.

Firstly, my fingers were getting numb; a quick change of gloves and some frantic rubbing by Dorje just about did the trick. Secondly, the body of Peter Kinloch. I had been warned but, knowing Peter from last year, it hit me quite suddenly. The body was bang in the middle of the route and we actually had to kick steps in around his head and away from his exposed, black hand which had been forced into a claw. *I'm sorry, Peter. I'm sorry you had to go through that. I'm sorry you didn't turn around. I'm sorry your young life ended here in this miserable and unforgiving place.* It just didn't seem right.

Dorje said, 'Let's go, Geordie. We can think about that when we get down. We must move or we get too cold.' He was right. There was nothing we or anybody else could do for Peter.

We made it to the base of the Second Step, changed oxygen bottles, increased our flow rate from two to four litres per minute and proceeded upwards. It was pitch black and, despite knowing from 2010 what lay beneath, the darkness masked my fears and through the cone of my headlight I could focus on what was ahead.

I watched as Dorje calmly worked his way up the ladder one rung at a time. Jaysen was close behind – I could see the flickering of his head torch and, through my beam, I noticed his distinctive purple rucksack. It was reassuring to see him and his Sherpa, Ang. Both he and Ang were people I trusted and got on with, so their presence gave me a boost and I knew that together we could keep going.

Dorje and I made it to the top of the Second Step, put our oxygen flow back to normal and continued along the gentle rise to the Third Step at 8,710m. I did not stop to take a video, or say anything, but my thoughts turned to 2010. It was at this point that my dream went up in smoke, as I saw Max and turned my back to the summit, having been told our turnaround time was fast approaching. I thought about this, and the contrast in how the days had gone. How much stronger I felt now, how much more support there was around me and how reassuring that it was still dark, only 4 a.m., as opposed to 9 a.m. the previous year.

Three more bodies lay ahead, including that of an Irish climber who died on the Third Step and whose body was still clipped onto the fixed rope. His family were not yet able to make a decision about whether they wanted it recovered or if it was to be moved out of sight, high on the mountain. Recovering bodies in this environment is manpower and resource-intensive, highly dangerous and therefore extremely expensive.

I did another radio check with Simon when I got above the Third Step: 'Simon, it's Geordie, we're on the summit slopes now and the sun is rising. Feeling good about this.' It was pleasing to hear his calm voice at the other end of the line, as it had been throughout the day when I radio checked at all the key points along the route. Doing this gave Simon accurate information to relay back to the UK, which allowed our families and friends at home to follow our progress. Simon responded with, 'Nice work, mate. You're doing well. Keep it up and speak when you get to the top.'

The sun rising high on a mountain is unbelievable. All night you plod along in your own world through a cone of light from your head torch, getting increasingly cold, but that all changes at dawn. It was the moment I was anticipating most, in a way – seeing the Himalayas light up in a magnificent orange glow. I could see the tops of the 8,000m-plus peaks such as Makalu and Cho Oyu way beneath us; no other mountain was as high as we were.

From the summit slopes, there is a spectacular traverse across the North Face of the mountain, as the Himalayas open up all around. I took a photo of Dorje here on a precarious little ledge. I knew I would always want to remember the exhilaration of that moment. It was the same North Face that had been a photo on my wall for all those years, that I had dreamed of, and there I was traversing it with the perfect companion.

After a small rocky section, the route switched back and began to open out. *I know it's near. Where is it? Where's the summit?* I felt good but just wanted to see my goal. It was tantalisingly close. Each false summit brought new hope, only to be crushed.

And then suddenly, with prayer flags fluttering in the wind, the summit appeared with not a soul on top. As we took each step, a little bit more detail came into focus and I welled up inside my oxygen mask. I knew I would make it. In ten minutes I would be standing there, on the summit of Everest.

I dragged my body over the tiny lip before the summit and a big hug from Dorje awaited me. I stood at 8,848m with the whole world beneath me.

I could not comprehend what was happening. I just sat down next to Dorje and cried. I barely moved for over an hour, just totally overwhelmed with emotion and deep in my own thoughts.

I was the highest person on earth at 6.30 a.m. on 26 May 2011 and had become the youngest Briton to climb the Seven Summits – the highest mountain on every continent.

There are times in life when you just want to bottle the whole experience. You want to keep everything about it forever – the people, the emotions, the atmosphere, the views. You just want to be able to look into that moment sometimes and remember. That was the moment.

The views are hard to put into words, as the world just

dropped away beneath where we stood. The sharp mountains of the Himalayas on one side and the rocky Tibetan plateau sprawled all across the other. Everything suddenly seemed so insignificant. I could hardly see Base Camp, all those miles away, and yet at Base Camp, all I could do was imagine what it was like to be up here.

Chris, our Canadian team leader, and Jaysen joined Dorje and I about fifteen minutes later and radioed to pass on the good news that we were on the summit. I asked to borrow his satellite phone as I had a few calls to make. Thankfully, despite the altitude, I remembered their phone numbers.

'Hi Dad, it's Geordie. I've made it. I'm on top of the world.' The reality of the moment brought tears to my eyes again. All the emotion that had been held in to get to this point just unloaded. 'I can't talk for long I'm afraid but I just wanted to say I'm thinking of you and can't wait to get home again.'

Dad said, 'Amazing, Geord. I don't know what to say. I'm so proud of you. Congratulations. Now get down safe, OK?'

'Hi Mum, it's me. I'm here. I'm at the summit.'

Mum tried to remain calm but I knew she must have been in a flat spin waiting for news. 'That's incredible! Well done. We're all so proud and can't wait to see you soon.'

'Hi Klara, guess what? I made it. I'm here at the summit of Everest!'

The response was more what I expected, 'Ahhh! No way, no

way. Yes! I love you so much. I knew you'd make it. I'm so proud of you, darling. Now please get back home to me.'

Three phone calls to three people I loved in different places. Unsurprisingly their phones went slightly mad after that as they began to text each other. My friends at St Andrews who had stayed up popped a bottle of champagne as soon as they heard the news. I had become the first St Andrews student ever to summit Everest and I proudly displayed their banner at the top.

After 45 minutes of sitting down in total awe and disbelief of where I was, I concluded I should probably record this moment. I took a few summit photos and a video.

Video Diary – 26 May 2011 – 7.15 a.m.

I'm at the summit of Mount Everest. It was a hard hard day and it's a long way down – a very important part to go down but the view from here is immense. Check out the view. Going round and round. I never thought I'd be here. What a place. I'm so happy. It's incredible. Jesus. This is amazing.

I was then joined at the summit by Ben and Andy. We hugged, high fived and each tried to savour this incredible feeling.

After 75 minutes on top, Dorje said, 'OK, Geordie, we must go now. You strong but not that strong. We can't stay forever.' He followed that up with a smile and added, 'Maybe next year.' I had made good time and felt relatively strong, but knew that my stint on the roof of the world was over.

26

A Promise

Better to have a live donkey than a dead lion.

Sir Ernest Shackleton

The vast majority of fatalities on mountains happen on the descent.

The physical movement of descending is more challenging certainly, but there are bigger issues than that, especially in the Death Zone. The more time spent above 8,000m means your body is physically wasting away. The sheer exhaustion of being on the move for so long takes hold eventually. One's oxygen supply begins to dwindle and when that goes, combined with darkness and an increase in winds on the Northeast Ridge, you are far more susceptible to frostbite. One's exposure to the altitude means HAPE and HACE, along with snow blindness, can become lethal afflictions that have caused the death of many great climbers. And that is all on top of the other great battle, the one between your ears. That little voice saying sit down and take a rest.

Making my way down was strenuous. So much of my physical and emotional energy, constrained until the summit, had suddenly been released. All the aches and pains my mind had bottled up immediately struck and bit hard. I passed Greg, Zac and Stephen near the summit slopes. I congratulated them, saying, 'Not far to go, I'll see you at the bottom,' before continuing downwards.

I would make as much progress as possible before stopping for a break. Dorje encouraged me to continue and together we staggered our way to High Camp. I had a litre of water waiting for me wrapped in my sleeping bag, so drank as much as possible. I grabbed the rest of my gear, packed my rucksack and forced myself, against all instincts, to keep going down.

I got to Camp 2, located my tent, removed my harness and crampons and clambered inside. I could hear the radio conversations, making me aware of where everyone was. I waited for a pause and let Simon know where I was for the night. I grabbed snow, used the little fluid I had left and began to get some water on the boil. I knew tomorrow would be the final push. With that in mind, I turned off my oxygen flow to save it for the descent.

Video Diary – 26 May 2011

To do my diary correctly I should probably do it after I get down which is now. I'm absolutely fucked. I'm knackered. My voice was going; I was coughing up blood but I got down to

*High Camp and am now at 7,800m. Man oh man what
a day.*

I had food and water prepared for Stephen's arrival, but
when he got there he was having all sorts of problems. He
could hardly work out who I was and imagined a radio
conversation that we didn't have. Altitude can have pretty
sudden hallucinogenic effects, as well as everything else,
and Stephen needed to get down fast. Chris plus a Sherpa
were with him and together, very wisely, they made it down
to ABC. It must have been a hell of a day, getting from the
summit down to 6,400m but, in the state he was in, with
severe HAPE, it was a very pragmatic decision that probably
saved his life.

I was without a tentmate again. I left my water bottle open
to allow the orange recovery powder to dissolve and
stupidly knocked the whole thing over, thus covering the
tent floor. I was pissed off. I lay out my roll mat and
proceeded to have the worst night of my life. I cannot recall
ever being so cold. My whole body was shivering violently,
forcing me awake, despite craving sleep. The orange liquid
beneath me began to freeze and I could see every puff of my
breath ascend into the roof of the tent. I felt bitterly alone. I
wished somebody else was in the tent with me to share body
heat. I was wearing every bit of clothing I had, and there was
nothing more I could do but wait out the night. I knew I
would not die but it was wretched. I missed home. I missed
my girlfriend. I made a promise to myself as I lay shivering
in that tent that I wouldn't go back to 8,000m. It was a long
and very lonely night.

I was comforted when the sun rose and was astounded by
the view as I peeked my head out the tent. I had most of my

clothes on already, so smashed the orange ice, remnants of Waterspillgate, off my harness, put on my oxygen mask again and headed down. It was at that moment that I thanked 'Day-Before Geordie' for saving the oxygen. Although I'd had a shit night, I did a few sums and worked out I had enough in the bottle to put it to the highest flow and get down in decent time. The plan worked, though it was still a tough few hours compelling my legs forward against the weaker part of my mind. I just had to keep going down and eventually I would get there.

I got to the tents at the North Col, made it down the Head-wall, thankfully without any whiteouts or crevasse rescues, past Crampon Corner, and then, finally, our tents came into view. An unimaginable feeling. Safety at last. I dumped my kit outside and walked through the doors to see Heather and Simon waiting. I had never been so happy to see them, shook their hands and just slumped into a nearby chair with total gratification and exhaustion.

I wrote to my family as soon as I could to let them know that I was safely at ABC.

Email to family – 27 May 2011

WOW!! What an incredible week. Everest, done. Seven Summits, done. I can't be dealing with any more 8,000m expeditions.

I feel exhausted right now. I think I need to chill the fuck out. My throat and back really hurt and taking 60 days or so away from the people I care about most isn't too healthy.

Feeling absolutely shattered but so so happy. More than

*four years after having this crazy plan and it is now over.
Cannot believe it.*

*The amount of thank yous I need to give is going to be
overwhelming. I am amazed this has concluded successfully.*

THANK YOU FOR EVERYTHING!!!!

Lots of love and speak properly when I'm in Kathmandu.

Xxx

It is quite rare to be able to share moments of great personal
joy and satisfaction with loved ones. The expeditions themselves were beyond their imaginations in many ways. To have
the opportunity to express how I felt at the summit via a sat
phone was truly special. I think I was so emotional speaking
to them for exactly that reason. I had rarely been able to
communicate the great moments and instead had to rely on
photos, videos and stories. They were with me every step of
the way. Not physically but emotionally and psychologically
they were always there for the best and worst moments.

By that afternoon the team had all made it down to ABC
with varying degrees of celebration, physical drain and frustration. Ten out of 15 of us had made the summit which,
compared to four out of 20 in 2010, was a superb effort.
Nothing is guaranteed up there, no inch is given to you by
the mountain or anything else. Regardless of the outcome,
we all suffered, and all worked hard. In the end, a mixture of
opportunity and resilience brought the summit to some
people not others.

Heading to that kind of place does takes its toll though, and
Ben's fingers were the most obvious evidence of that. He had

committed to climbing the First Step with just thin gloves to assist his dexterity but the fresh snow had frozen solid, meaning he was suffering from frostbite on one of his hands.

As he said afterwards, 'I now had the difficult decision to make, do I go back down and try and save my fingers, or do I carry on to the summit and risk losing them all? I decided to carry on toward the summit. The decision resulted in me losing the distal phalanx of two fingers when I got back home. I don't regret it one bit because, to me, it was worth it!'

Greg said about that summit, 'It was only a few minutes but it's one event that you will certainly remember and treasure for the rest of your life.'

He was right. Everest would always remain with us.

Everest is a hugely solitary venture, in that nobody is going to force you to the top. However, we were extremely lucky to have people around whom we trusted and who, at different times in the expedition, gave strength to others. In Jaysen's words, 'The fact that ten of us made it to the top was a result of that team effort.'

It was the small moments of selflessness that created that trust and cohesion. It was Zac's kindness at Base Camp when I was recovering from my food poisoning in Kathmandu. It was Jacob climbing with me stride for stride up the North Ridge when I was struggling. It was Stephen's cooking at Camp 2 and Jaysen being behind me most of summit day and, unbeknownst to him, giving me the conviction to keep going forwards. It was speaking to Simon on the radio during summit day and hearing his calm voice offering encouragement and optimism.

Then, of course, there was Dorje. He was a pillar of strength for me throughout the expedition and kept his word. From the moment he saw me, he promised he would take me to the summit. All the way through the climb, to his warm embrace on top of the world, his kindness and selflessness was unmatched. I probably wouldn't have made it without him. What a guy.

27

CONTENTMENT

To meet yourself is one of the toughest things to do in life and that is also why it is so important...

Erling Kagge

When I left Base Camp in 2010 my body felt hollow as Everest slowly disappeared from view to a mere speck in the distance. So tantalisingly close and yet so very far.

My perspective leaving in 2011 had fundamentally altered. We drove away and the mountain retained its majestic beauty but something was different. I had spent many months in the shadows of *Chomolungma*. I had spent all but three days of that time looking up at the summit and dreaming of being the tiny spec in the distance, only visible through the strongest of telescopes. I dreamed of being the person on the summit gazing in utter disbelief at the world below. I dreamed of straining with every fibre in my body to be given the opportunity briefly to experience what it was like to stand at the summit.

Leaving the mountain was not a hollow feeling but neither was it a whole one. I felt fulfilled and satisfied, but, equally, I felt a sense of loss. Perhaps it was the loss of the pressure that I had imposed upon myself for all these years, or the loss of a great adversary. Perhaps it was the loss of ignorant wonder at what it would be like to summit Everest. It had dictated my thoughts and actions for such a long time and I think I knew I would not be back anytime soon. I knew that my stint on Everest had come to its conclusion and that also spelled the end of a chapter of my life.

Returning to Kathmandu after the harsh world of the mountains in all their hostility and purity was a bit of a shock. The simplicity and escapism of being on an expedition had ended. Instead of books and time on our hands, we had mobile phones and traffic to dodge. In a place I had such fondness for, I felt uneasy, as though my mind was still hoping to peer out of my tent in the morning and examine the snow whipping off the high slopes. The disorder of the city was in utter contrast to the clarity of the mountains.

I went to the hotel, had a shower and, unlike in 2010, when the free-flowing water had caused an emotional fault line to quiver, I felt relaxed and whole. The sweat, grime and dirt fell away from me. Cleansed and freshly shaved, a sense of serene satisfaction overcame anything else.

Instead of the deep melancholy I'd felt when I had a beer with Matt and Pete to celebrate their success in 2010, I was calm and could share fond memories of the expedition with friends. We sat and laughed at our faces without beards and our heads without hats, goggles and sunburn. We mocked each other about mistakes we made up the mountain, the geriatric speed of some of our summit attempts, our pathetic cooking attempts up high and the utter relief of seeing everyone at ABC. Our night ended in a tuk tuk race around Kathmandu – recommended for the thrill but not for safety or sanity. Morale was high as we celebrated what had been an extraordinary experience.

On the plane from Kathmandu to London, the captain came over the tannoy and announced, 'If you look to your right now, you will see Mount Everest, the highest mountain in the world.' Unlike in 2010 when I could not bear the thought of looking at the mountain again, I turned my head to the right. I gazed deeply at the magnificence of Everest and thought how blessed I was, for one very insignificant hour in the history of the world, to have been able to stand there and look at the world beneath me.

I took my baggage trolley and the automatic doors of the arrivals hall at Heathrow opened before me. Within a matter of seconds, I had my beautiful girlfriend, Klara, charging up screaming in delight, wearing shorts and a red T-shirt with a picture of Everest and the words 'TEAM GEORDIE' imprinted on it. I twirled her around and gave her, my sisters and Mum enormous hugs. They all had matching T-shirts, congratulations balloons and banners.

Even now, I walk through the arrivals gate and often think back to that moment. I think back to the level of genuine excitement and joy we all felt embracing after two months that would be seared deeply into our memories.

How it contrasted to 2010 when a skinny disheartened kid came through those doors and hugged his family out of love and a deep need to be consoled.

Now I could celebrate with them, as in many ways it was their journey as much as mine. They were there from the beginning, never doubting, always believing; supporting and never ridiculing. I shared the journey with them from start to finish. Maybe not every aspect of it – the alcoves of my confused mind were not always able to share some of my more personal fears and issues – but pretty much. They were the ones I emailed when I was scared, angry or happy. They were the ones who had to keep me motivated when I could not get sponsorship. They had to pick up the pieces when I failed to summit in 2010 and spent months of introspection to get myself vaguely motivated to do anything. They were there at the other end of a telephone from the summit of Everest. Finally, they were there at the airport when I returned from Nepal having completed my dreams. None of it would have been possible without their love and support.

I returned home to a beautiful British summer. As in 2010 I went to the fridge, grabbed a beer, rolled a cigarette, went to the garden and sat in a deckchair with Bob Dylan playing. Lao Tzu said, 'If you are depressed, you are living in the past.

If you are anxious, you are living in the future. If you are at peace, you are living in the present.'

At that time, I think I'd achieved what I'd been seeking all along. I had realised the real dream that had manifested itself on those seven mountains. It was not about breaking any records, it was not about Everest and it was not about the Seven Summits. They were hostile, beautiful and amazing places I was fortunate to visit. The real dream was to find silence instead of the noise in my head. I needed silence within to meet myself and find the answers. The real dream was to find inner contentment. Right then, according to Lao Tzu's definition, I was living in the present and was in a state of peace.

The love of nature is what draws people to the mountains. Mountains can represent calm, tranquillity and simplicity. They can be a means of escape from everyday life, a way to find clarity of thought and peace of mind. Edmund Hillary said he felt on Everest 'like an ant in a land made for giants'. Big mountains do that, they demand humility and respect.

Nobody can control the character and nature of a mountain. We try to put parameters in place for our safety but that very real element of purity in nature is why people love being there. We love looking up in bewilderment at the seemingly unreachable summit of a mountain and then, in total awe, gazing down at the beauty of the world from the top.

Robert Macfarlane wrote *Mountains of the Mind* about the human draw to mountains:

Most of us exist for most of the time in worlds which are humanly arranged, themed and controlled. One forgets that there are environments which do not respond to the flick of a switch or the twist of a dial, and which have their own rhythms and orders of existence. Mountains correct this amnesia. By speaking of greater forces than we can possibly invoke, and by confronting us with greater spans of time than we can possibly envisage, mountains refute our excessive trust in the man-made. They pose profound questions about our durability and the importance of our schemes. They induce, I suppose, a modesty in us.

People question from the comfort of their armchairs at home how Everest has changed over the years. They say commercialisation has ruined the spirit of mountaineering. They say that climbing Everest is easy and that it's like having an escalator to the top due to increased numbers and levels of support. However, I am not a hugely experienced and accomplished mountaineer by any means and would never claim to be. I will never be Reinhold Messner, Chris Bonnington or Doug Scott.

I dared to dream when I was a naïve 17-year-old suffering from bulimia that I could climb the highest mountain on every continent. I dreamed as big as I could and people scoffed at the idea. People laughed at a kid with a dream because they did not believe it was possible. For years I worked relentlessly to make that dream a reality. I sacrificed my social life and time at university, hampered relationships, friendships and much else. I had times when I never thought it would be possible because of financial constraints, logistics or altitude sickness.

Everest remained the dream. Not because it was the hardest or the most technical but because of what it represented to me. I did not care what other people or what the media thought about how hard it was, or how it had changed from the 'glory days'. I did not care that people made assumptions as to why I wanted to climb. This was my dream.

I have been truly humbled and exposed on that mountain. It made me find reserves I never thought I had. I witnessed astonishing levels of fortitude, perseverance, selflessness and skill. I saw the raw and undistorted emotion of grown men and women pushed to their limit. I witnessed first-hand the degree to which people were willing to push themselves in order to achieve the satisfaction of standing on the summit of a mountain.

That mountain taught me more about human fragility, human weaknesses and strengths, more than any other experience in my life. It was a true test of one's morality when life and death were genuinely very possible outcomes. It showed egotism, selfishness and arrogance, but matched that with kindness, respect and love. It brought about fear, but then challenged people to combat that with unprecedented levels of resourcefulness and courage.

Everest will never be the same mountain it was when George Mallory unlocked the door to the Northeast Ridge. It will never be the same as when Edmund Hillary and Tenzing Norgay shuffled their way up that little chimney, walked along a ridge and hoisted an ice axe in the air in 1953.

Everest will, however, continue to represent more than that.

It changes people's lives – it changed my life. It challenges the climbers that step onto its slopes. It forces them to seek *sisu* deep within and gives them an insight into the magnitude and power of human and physical nature.

It gives people hope, and above everything else, it gives people a reason to dream.

POSTSCRIPT

In April 2014, I found out that Sherpa Dorje Khatri was one of 16 people killed in one of the worst disasters ever recorded on Mount Everest.

Dorje was the leader of Nepal's trade union of Sherpas and a committed defender of the environment. Together on the summit of Everest in 2011, we stood with the International Trade Union Confederation (ITUC) flag as part of a global mobilisation for action on climate change.

Hearing about Dorje's death was shocking and sad. Like many who have had the pleasure of being in the mountains with him, I found it was impossible not to be drawn to his enthusiasm and kindness. His passion for mountains and for the people who climb them was infectious but, above all, it was his selflessness that moved me. He had such deep caring for other people. I was blessed to have climbed, and reached the summit of Everest, with such a wonderful man. I treasure the moments we shared and will remain forever grateful to him for helping me and many others achieve their dreams. It would not have been possible without him.

Dorje died aged 46 and had summited Everest nine times. He was a proud father and husband and his loss is still felt strongly back in Nepal.

ACKNOWLEDGEMENTS

To my family:

You shared the journey with me from beginning to end. You were always there and this book is as much about thanking you as anything else. You supported me through everything and believed in me while I was putting my thoughts to paper.

I would not have got here without your love and support.

To my friends:

My list of people to thank just continued to grow due to the immense selflessness of others during this journey. Climbing those mountains was not an individual effort. Your friendships allowed me to grow and allowed me to achieve my dreams.

Particular mentions have to go to Freddie and Linnea who stood by me through the good times and bad. It was not easy but never underestimate the strength you provided.

Genevieve, I would never have started to write this journey without your love, passion and kindness.

To my sponsors:

Stuart Mitchell, Philip Magor, Geoff Morris and Andrew Rome. At different times in the journey, you all rescued a sinking ship and gave it a chance to stay afloat.

It would not have been possible without you taking a plunge and I hope I repaid your faith.

To my teammates:

There's so many of you that have had such a massive impact on my climbing knowledge, expertise and personal growth.

We saw each other through some great times, some pretty bleak periods and everything in between up there.

Unique places attract unique people and it was a genuine privilege to share those moments with you.

To those who assisted with the book:

Jen, my editor, for your amazing work with the ropey draft I handed over to you. Olive, for your wonderful artistic talents. Henry and Pip, for your sage advice and wise words. Charlie and Bonita, for blazing a trail and giving me the conviction to follow this through.

To those who supported my Kickstarter campaign:

I was so touched by all your generosity and kind words. Thank you for making this book happen.

Spirit of Exploration

Jessica Chan, Emily Dehn, Digby Don, Alastair Ferrans, Douglas and Agnes Ferrans, Freddie fforde, Guy Fillipich, Laura Fisher, Harry Geaves, George Carroll, Howard and Zoe Johnston, Aaron Lee, Linnea Lundquist, Philip Magor, Bonita Norris, Chris and Joan Rea, Henry Reddaway, Gilly Stewart, Hugh Stewart, Amelia Watson, Louise and Michael Wigley, Sinead and Sid Wilson, Wingfield's - Quality Adventure Goods, The Rory McDonagh Trust

Pursuit of Adventure

Jane and John Andrews, Charles Arnot, Jack Barker, Olivia L'Estrange-Bell, Paul and Susie Boissier, Alberto Brignone, Hannah Brown, Steve Burton, Darcy Carlin Carnegie, Joshua Carter, Oscar Churton, Moreton 'Chief' Cullimore, Gethin Davies, Julian Everard, Rob Everard, Joe Fellows, Geraint Fisher, Lucy Gordon, Simon and Jackie Gordon, Jamie Gray, Will Griffith, Cameron Gubbins, Nina Haanes Hessen, Matthew Hazlett, Tor Henman, Adam Hodges, Deborah Hudson, Thomas Hunter, Simon James, Thomas P.O. Jebsen, Naheed Jivraj, Flora and Henry Kay, Anthony Kilby, Jane and John Lavers, Harry Mackarness, Fred Mahon, William and Cilla Massey, Orna McEntee, Frances Mitchell, Roger and Caroline Morgan-Grenville, Edward and Didi Nicholson, Tare Nyabadza, Tom Parry, Freddy Paske, Rob Perera, Jonathan Quicke, Julia Rea, Marianne Sæland, Kaja Sæland Sandvig, Pip and Ben Saunders, David Scott, Tom Skelding, Olivia Sims, Gareth Slade-Jones, Victoria Stewart, Peter Sunnucks, Freddie Vicker-Craddock, Jack Warrillow, Heather Warwick, Clive Woodman

GLOSSARY

Bivouac – usually temporary encampment under little or no shelter. Also known as a 'bivvy'.

Crampon – spiked metal device that attaches to a mountain climber's boot and provides sure footing on ice and snow.

Crevasse – huge, deep crack in the ice of a glacier.

Couloir – steep gully or gorge frequently filled with snow or ice.

Dexamethasone – pharmaceutical drug used in the treatment of HACE as well as HAPE. It is commonly carried on mountain climbing expeditions to help climbers deal with altitude sickness. Also known as 'Dex'.

Glacier – large, slow-moving mass of ice in a high mountain valley, formed by the accumulation of compacted snow as it moves down from higher altitudes.

High altitude cerebral edema (HACE) – severe, and often fatal, form of altitude sickness involving swelling of the brain.

High altitude pulmonary edema (HAPE) – serious form of altitude sickness involving fluid accumulation in the lungs.

Hypothermia – potentially fatal fall of body temperature below 35C.

Jet stream – high-speed wind current in the earth's upper troposphere, the lowest layer of the atmosphere at six to 12 miles high. The current typically travel west to east in both hemispheres between 80–140mph, between 9,000m and 12,000m above the earth's surface.

Jumar – most common type of ascender, a mechanical safety device used to ascend on a rope when climbing mountains. The device locks onto the climber's ropes and is attached to one's harness. As the climber moves up the rope, the device slides up, gripping the rope to prevent the climber from sliding backward.

Karabiner – D-shaped clip with a hinge used to connect ropes in mountain climbing.

Lama – in Tibetan Buddhism, a spiritual leader or monk.

North Col – mountain pass in the Himalayas between mounts Everest and Changtse. The pass or col forms a saddle between the mountains and was the site of Camp 1 at 7,000m.

Second Step – 40m rock step, and the major obstacle, on the Northeast Ridge of Everest located at 8,610m.

Serac – tall peak of ice on the surface of a glacier, usually formed where crevasses intersect.

Sherpa – person of the ethnic group of the same name that